FUTURESHOP

FUTURESHOP

How the New Auction Culture Will
Revolutionize the Way We Buy, Sell,
and Get the Things We REALLY Want

DANIEL NISSANOFF

The Penguin Press
New York
2006

THE PENGUIN PRESS
Published by the Penguin Group
Penguin Group (USA) Inc., 375 Hudson Street, New York, New York 10014, U.S.A. •
Penguin Group (Canada), 90 Eglinton Avenue East, Suite 700, Toronto, Ontario, Canada
M4P 2Y3 (a division of Pearson Penguin Canada Inc.) • Penguin Books Ltd, 80 Strand,
London WC2R 0RL, England • Penguin Ireland, 25 St. Stephen's Green, Dublin 2, Ireland
(a division of Penguin Books Ltd) • Penguin Books Australia Ltd, 250 Camberwell Road,
Camberwell, Victoria 3124, Australia (a division of Pearson Australia Group Pty Ltd) •
Penguin Books India Pvt Ltd, 11 Community Centre, Panchsheel Park, New Delhi –
110 017, India • Penguin Group (NZ), Cnr Airborne and Rosedale Roads, Albany,
Auckland 1310, New Zealand (a division of Pearson New Zealand Ltd) • Penguin Books
(South Africa) (Pty) Ltd, 24 Sturdee Avenue, Rosebank, Johannesburg 2196, South Africa

Penguin Books Ltd, Registered Offices:
80 Strand, London WC2R 0RL, England

First published in 2006 by The Penguin Press,
a member of Penguin Group (USA) Inc.

ISBN 1-59420-077-7

This book is printed on acid-free paper. ∞

Printed in the United States of America
1   3   5   7   9   10   8   6   4   2
Designed by Lee Fukui

To Amy and Asher

CONTENTS

FUTURESHOP

INTRODUCTION

I was visiting with my friend Anna, a twenty-nine-year-old interior decorator, not long ago on a warm summer afternoon when the doorbell rang unexpectedly. Anna disappeared to see who it was, and I continued to chat with Jamie, her new husband, about their Caribbean honeymoon until his wife interrupted us.

"Jamie, we got another one," Anna called, resignation audible in her voice, from the hallway, before she returned carrying a heavy box with large Crate and Barrel labels prominently displayed on all sides. They opened the package with none of the excitement one might expect of a young couple surveying their spoils to discover that Anna's cousin David and his wife, Sara, had sent them a portable cast-iron grill. Jamie quickly closed the package up again and carried it to the closet, where he added it to a teeming collection of similar boxes from Tiffany, Williams-Sonoma, and Target.

Most of the couples I know who register for wedding gifts think of the process as a fabulous shopping spree on someone else's account. They let their imaginations run wild. Should we get napkins in blue or green? Should the hors d'oeuvres platter be gold or silver? Birch or maple salad bowls? "Put us down for the stainless steel version . . . make that two!" No longer just for place settings and linens, wedding registrations have evolved to the point where couples can now add tents, lumber, and stereos to their wish lists.

Anna and Jamie, however, had a different kind of wish list. They've been into gourmet cooking for years, so their kitchen is already stocked with coordinating plates, and all the spring pans, Italian bottle stoppers, microplane zest graters, and professional-quality slicing, grinding, and pureeing appliances they could ever need. They've lived together for a couple of years, so their bathroom already has matching plush towels, and they're very happy with their Egyptian cotton sheets. They simply didn't need most of the wedding gifts they received, as much as they appreciated the generosity of those who sent them. What they really wanted, instead, to get their married life off to a good start was something different.

Anna and Jamie didn't want crystal. They wanted a condo. But of course, there's no real trade-off there, between wedding gifts and the down payment it takes to buy an apartment—or is there?

Anna's original plan regarding wedding gifts was to forgo the registry process altogether and tell anyone who asked them what they'd like for their wedding that their preference would be cash.

Jamie's mother hadn't liked that idea and convinced her future daughter-in-law that registering was the right thing to do. It would be risky not to register because inevitably some people would prefer to give an actual gift and they were likely to get stuck with a bunch of things that they would never have chosen for themselves.

So Anna was persuaded—and a month after the wedding her closets were filled with things she'd chosen but didn't really need, or even want. And to add insult to injury, she and Jamie had finally stumbled across a new development downtown with an apartment that was just what they were looking for.

Why couldn't they just take the presents back? I wondered. Certainly, their friends would understand, and be happy that they'd helped them afford the one thing they truly wanted.

Of course, they'd thought of that, but most retailers that provide wedding registries will accept returns only if you're making exchanges, or for store credit, they told me.

What they hadn't thought of—probably because they didn't know—was that, today, there's a brisk market for store credit to prominent national retail stores if you know where to go. Store credit may not be as good as cash to the stores that issue it, but it might be worth just that—cash—to someone else.

An analysis of thousands of gift card transactions on eBay reveals that store credits to popular retailers fetch very close to their face value in the secondary market, where they usually sell for 80 to 90 percent of their original cost, depending on the store and the amount. A quick search found that just the day before Anna, Jamie, and I were talking, a card for $500 of store credit at Target sold for $450, a $175 Tiffany gift card fetched $135, and a $200 Crate and Barrel exchange credit receipt got $188.99, shipping included.

In the booming world of secondary markets—dominated by eBay—buyers are actually competing vigorously for store credit in order to save a few dollars on purchases at their favorite stores. In some cases, the buyer pool is so robust that store credit on eBay is just about as good as cash, and generally, the higher the dollar value, the lower the proportional discount will be, so that, in fact, the discount is substantively not that much different from paying a commission to a currency exchange when you change your money in a foreign country.

Would they, I asked Anna and Jamie, be willing to exchange their presents for cash on the secondary market if they could get eighty cents on the dollar?

Indeed they would.

The three of us set out on a reverse shopping spree. Anna's cheeks reddened at one return counter when the clerk asked why she wanted to return all her gifts. Caught off guard, she mumbled something about the wedding having been called off (Jamie was waiting in the car), after which the clerk obliged and issued her a card worth $4,500 of store credit. By the time we got to the next store, she just said she was moving to LA and wanted to buy directly from the local branch when she got there. It worked.

We ended the day with more than $15,000 in store credit cards.

Anna has an eBay account, but she had previously only bought a few hard-to-find household items through the site over the years and had never even thought of auctioning anything herself. Because she was such an infrequent user, she didn't have any so-called customer "feedback" ratings from the site, which would assure her potential customers that she was a trustworthy seller who would deliver the goods as promised and in a timely manner. The kinds of shoppers who frequent eBay have enough experience to know that they'd rather buy a $4,500 item from someone who's sanctioned by other users through positive feedback, so Anna wasn't likely to get maximum value for her gift cards if she posted them on her own. So I suggested she let a more proficient (and well-reputed) middleman deal with it for her. We took the gift cards to a popular local dropshop, a store that takes your items and sells them for you in online auctions. Anna filled out some quick forms, which gave the store's employees—experts in the orchestration of online auctions—a license to arrange and execute the processes.

A few weeks later, Anna called to tell me that her cards had sold for more than $12,000. She and Jamie were thrilled. And significantly closer to having the money they'd need for a down payment. Once Anna saw how easy it was to sell the cards through the dropshop, she looked through her closets to see what other unwanted or neglected possessions she could sell for even more cash to put toward the condo. The following week, she made three separate trips to the dropshop, bringing in everything from seasons-old pieces of clothing to the electronic organizer she'd never learned how to use to her childhood Barbie doll collection.

I had created a monster.

·   ·   ·

WHAT WAS MOST surprising to me about the whole process was how novel the concept of selling their unwanted possessions was to my friends. Anna and Jamie are young and intelligent and ambitious people. They read the papers and have wide social networks filled with like-minded professionals. Jamie is always suggesting that we try the new restaurants that, two weeks later, are booked solid for months, and Anna always knows what colors will be "in" next season. But even so, though they'd certainly heard of eBay and had bought books online at Amazon, they were almost completely unaware that there was such a robust marketplace out there, just waiting to let them turn the things they owned but didn't want into other things that they did. They were almost entirely oblivious to the phenomenon that I've spent most of my professional career trying to exploit.

There are a lot of reasons why so many people haven't even dipped their toes into the world of eBay, or any of the many other online secondary markets, yet. I'll take a hard look at those reasons in a bit. But the first point to make is that it's time for those who haven't explored the opportunities of the online auction world yet to plunge in. And for those who've been avid eBayers for years, or are in any kind of retail business, or who track consumer behavior, it's essential to know that a remarkable transformation in the secondary markets is now well under way.

A PARADIGM SHIFT

This is a book about how we behave as consumers today, and how we will behave in the future. Right now, in this moment, we live in an "accumulation nation," a consumer culture based on a system of legacy values that was forged by our ancestors in a different time. These values have taught us to acquire new things and then grow old with them. We are socially engineered to think that "used" is inferior or bad. And, with a few very specific exceptions, we are generally loath or unable to purge our possessions, even as their value or utility begins to wane. Our cluttered attics and garages tell this sad story of how our society lives today in its archaic ways.

But we're changing.

From Main Street to the upper echelons of society we are beginning to accept and will soon vigorously adopt a new lifestyle, one predicated on the norm of temporary ownership and marked by the continuous replacement of our personal possessions. Owning and selling things secondhand will become second nature. I like to think of this practice as "auction culture" because it's the auction platform that's so far been the catalyst for this behavior. But whatever label ultimately sticks to it, this transition will have a profound impact on our culture and values. It will not only shape the future of consumer behavior, it will also have tremendous implications for the business world.

We often think that we've already been through one social revolution—the digital revolution—and that we've probably experienced enough sweeping change for our lifetimes. The Internet has, of course, had a meaningful impact on our lives, in the way we gather and process information, in the way we communicate with each other, but it's not yet had a significant impact on our ethos as consumers. Sure, we can buy things online and we might save a little bit of time and money, but has that convenience really affected our society and culture? Ask anyone who works in the consumer sales force from Saks Fifth Avenue to Wal-Mart and they'll assure you that it hasn't.

The next generation of digital marketplaces, led by eBay, is about to change that. To date, eBay has made a lot of noise. Offering millions of products in hundreds of categories ranging from antiques to video games, eBay has created a venue for buying and selling previously owned items that is miles wide. However, despite attracting more than 150 million users and processing more than $80 million in daily transactions, eBay's marketplace is still only inches deep. While novel, convenient, often fun to use, and even addicting to some, eBay has barely made a dent on our mainstream culture as consumers. The fact is that so far it has failed to offer the kind of true liquidity needed to fuel a cultural revolution, meaning consistently efficient trading that yields true market value for the goods sold. The stock market is the model of liquidity; thus far eBay is far off that mark.

But the critical inflection point is upon us. As eBay approaches new levels of depth and breadth, it is beginning to create a new ecosystem—along with its subsidiaries, competitors, and off-line complements—that will rapidly accelerate the liquidity of the consumer-to-consumer marketplace and make it easier for mainstream society to access it. The multitude of valuable services created by freshly minted start-ups feeding on this ecosystem will fuel a new level of buying and selling activity at a higher rate than we've seen before. It will ripple throughout the global economy.

The aftershocks of this phenomenon will cause a dramatic shift in behavior whose repercussions will be stitched into the fabric of our society, culture, and business for years to come.

This shift will redefine socially accepted norms for consumer buying and selling behavior. We will soon live in a world where the norm is to sell our iPods after using them for a year. Or you'll sell your $800 Jimmy Choo shoes after wearing them twice. Cell phone companies will automatically send us the newest, most high-tech mobile phone every six months. We'll essentially be leasing Rolex watches instead of buying them. The new paradigm will change the very meaning of brand value and alter fundamental methods of marketing across the range of most consumer products.

In the same stroke, auction culture will create a universe of new business opportunities. Unprepared companies, no matter how old or lofty their pedigrees, will fall behind while companies that creatively embrace the new inclinations will surge ahead. A new breed of "facilitators" will emerge to provide an array of innovative services that will lubricate the newfound market. Some of them will partner with the world's largest companies, helping them manage and protect their brands while navigating the treacherous waters of the used-goods markets. Other facilitators will become trusted sources for consumers, acting as personal lifestyle consultants while disseminating information on when and what to buy and sell.

This new system of checks and balances will shine a bright light on how consumers choose brands. It will reinforce the importance of a brand in a virtual mall where reading the label on a digital photograph becomes the closest thing to touching and feeling what you buy. Yet at the same time, it will shake up the status quo by reshuffling brand values according to how well a product actually sells in the secondary market. As an "informed consumer" you will choose the brand of your new handbag based on how much it will fetch on eBay next year, which corresponds to how much it will really cost you to own it up until then.

Corporate culture will seal the fate of many organizations as they square off to deal with the various forces of change. Brave companies will embrace them and benefit. Pompous brand owners will fight them and lose to forces of nature bigger than they are and too powerful to resist. Stubborn corporations will ignore them and wake up in the not too distant future to find that their brands have eroded. Organizations that understand the new dynamics between the secondary and primary markets will strengthen their products inherently, and in so doing increase customer loyalty.

In the end, anyone who understands how to maximize the value-to-utility life cycle of their possessions will be rewarded with a more prosperous but less costly lifestyle. Plainly, we'll live better, cheaper—the incidental but significant benefit of a more efficient world.

I'm convinced about how dramatic and profound this shift will be because I've spent the last two years working to build a business that's at the center of this new world. Portero, the company I co-founded in 2004, is a service business that facilitates participation in the online secondary markets for sellers of luxury-class items, such as jewelry, watches, designer clothing, fine housewares, art, and collectibles, who don't want to go through the hassle of selling on eBay or any of the other marketplaces themselves. We emphasize convenience, visiting our clients' homes, appraising and authenticating their items. And we help them capture maximum value for their goods by professionally managing the sales processes and merchandising the items in a high-end manner to potential buyers. It's a service similar to the one Anna found at her local dropshop, but with a particular expertise and for a specific market. An explosion of such facilitator businesses is under way, and many more kinds of innovative businesses that will make trading online easier, more reliable, and more lucrative are soon to come. I'll describe these developments in more detail later in the book.

I'm also convinced of the magnitude of change to come because of my previous experience building a B2B Internet company called PartMiner. That experience taught me that the power of facilitating the trade of items that one party doesn't need or want anymore to another party who is seeking them out is an economic juggernaut, once you get the mechanism right. When I founded PartMiner, my first thought was that a digital secondary marketplace could make certain kinds of manufacturing businesses more efficient, so I created a business-to-business Internet exchange called the Free Trade Zone, which served the semiconductor industry. From my experience working as an attorney and advising companies in corporate reorganization, I knew that one of the most debilitating problems facing many manufacturers of technologically sophisticated products was that they weren't always able to buy the very specific electronics component parts that they needed to build their products when they needed them. I also knew that other manufacturers were often left holding large inventories of parts that they couldn't use and no longer needed. By creating a trading platform on which the two sides could find each other, we could solve both their problems, and that's just what PartMiner did. And we did it so well that by 2000 we had raised more than $100 million and reached a valuation in excess of half a billion dollars.

You might read that and conclude that the manufacturers were just bad businessmen. How could a multibillion-dollar cell phone maker like Nokia be caught short of a crucial component or a behemoth manufacturer like Intel be stuck with too many of them? Why couldn't they agree to make and buy the right amount in the first place? In a perfect world, they could. But in this world, chip makers require long lead times to fulfill large orders, which have to be placed months in advance of delivery. Nobody, not even Nokia, can know exactly what its needs will be six months out. A new, better chip might come onto the market from someone else in the interim and Nokia decides it needs to buy that one instead, or Intel could find a way to produce a similar chip more cost effectively and migrate its resources to that one, discontinuing the previous model.

People are like manufacturers in this way—they don't always know what they're going to need or want in the future. Their tastes change, unpredictably over time, and so does their corresponding demand for "stuff." They find themselves stuck with old things they can no longer use, and they search desperately for new things they feel they can't live without.

What eBay and the host of other online exchanges do, fundamentally, is help bridge the gap between supply and demand among people. As these exchanges continue to evolve, more and more buyers have come to these markets to compete with each other, prices have begun to climb, and the availability of desirable goods has skyrocketed. That's the economic juggernaut that will drive the shift to the auction culture.

In just about a decade, these exchanges have brought a level of convenience and efficiency and breadth to the secondary markets that is completely unprecedented. Today, the secondary market for everyday items like cameras, shoes, handbags, and watches is vast. Not only does supply generally exist to meet demand, but sellers are beginning to get good value for secondhand items. Trading in the secondary markets is quickly becoming a mainstream activity and, for many, a healthy form of generating income.

What I've seen personally through my business, and what the initial success and now exponential growth of exchanges like eBay indicate, is that gaining access to the secondary markets can be a life-altering and life-improving opportunity. The more value we are able to retrieve from the things in our lives that no longer serve a productive purpose, the more value we'll have to invest in things that will. It's a simple concept, but we still have a distance to go before it really becomes the new primary basis for consumer behavior.

For one thing, eBay and other secondary trading platforms are far from perfect and substantial changes will be required before the majority of people will want to become full-fledged traders, selling as well as buying. The shift won't happen until that balances out. As of now, secondary-market buyers outnumber sellers by orders of magnitude. For example, only about 5 percent of those who have bought items on eBay have ever sold anything on the site. That's in large part because the selling process remains more cumbersome than casual users are willing to tolerate. And, while there are robust secondary markets—both digital and non— for some large, high-priced items like automobiles, the secondary-market audience has generally remained wary of spending large sums in a marketplace that is relatively unproven, unregulated, and unsafe compared to primary channels. With higher bids come higher risks, especially the risk of being a victim of fraud. I'll discuss these and a number of other problems that are currently barriers to entry for so many people later in the book, as well as the solutions under way to address those problems.

More fundamental to auction culture truly taking off will be a change in consciousness among consumers. Maximizing the utilities of the secondary marketplace will require, for one thing, a change in the way we think about ownership and about our attachment to the goods we buy. It will also require convincing consumers en masse that the liquidity they can find for their used goods online—the trading power they'll be able to depend on—and the supply of high-quality used goods to be bought outweigh any hesitancy they have about becoming involved with the used-goods trade. After all, the trade in used goods has a long and somewhat sordid history, and there's still a stigma to buying something someone else has owned—unless, of course, it's a collectible, an airplane, or possibly a yacht.

A thriving community of online traders got addicted to eBay years ago, and maybe you're one of them, but the fact is that many, many more consumers have not, and no one will be able to reap the maximum potential rewards of the auction culture until the masses join in.

So before turning to the state-of-the-art developments under way in the post-eBay economy, it's important to take a look at the old ways of thinking that will have to change, and also at the big liquidity payoff that the online auction sites offer that no other used-goods marketplace of the past could provide.

1 PRIMITIVE VALUES
The Accumulation Nation

Browse through the average American closet or garage or attic and you will find a mass of clutter: brick-sized, museum-worthy calculators from the 1970s, old cameras and coffeemakers, hulking exercise equipment that hasn't been touched in years, clothes that don't fit or are desperately out of style. We're a nation of pack rats: itchy to acquire, loath to relinquish.

TO HAVE IS TO HOARD

Merriam-Webster describes the pack rat as "a bushy-tailed rodent of western North America that has well-developed cheek pouches and that hoards food and miscellaneous objects." The animals hoard because it's in their DNA. Maybe we hoard, in part, for the same reason.

The impulse to hoard probably has its roots in our earliest days. There's a reason why we call our predecessors "hunter-gatherers." It was only about twelve thousand years ago that our ancestors were finally able to gather more than they could consume. Once that finally happened, people learned to trade things they no longer needed—extra portions of meat or ears of corn—for other things they wanted—a new hunting knife or a warm pelt. Over time, acquiring goods became an indicator of status.

But we've not only been bred to prize new possessions, we've also been taught to want to get all of the value that we can out of them. And, in addition, many of the things we buy take on an emotional value—we want to keep them because they remind us of good memories or a stage in our lives.

All of those reasons—symbolism, frugality, and emotion—sound practical enough. It's sensible to keep things that are expected to rise in value over time or possessions that are particularly sentimental. So what's wrong with manifesting our attachment to our belongings by holding on to them?

APPARENT VALUE, EMOTIONAL VALUE

There's nothing inherently wrong with feeling emotional about our possessions—in many cases, we do it with good reason. We all should have relics of our past and of our families' pasts—a great-grandmother's candlesticks, a grandfather's pocket watch, our own or our children's first pairs of shoes or baseball mitts—to the extent that it gives us pleasure or fulfills an emotional need. They teach us about our predecessors, inspire feelings of connectedness, remind us of who we are. Those types of possessions have a sentimental value that we—and, hopefully, our descendants—are right to quantify emotionally.

But emotional value is finite. When pressed, we would probably part with many of these things if the reward were great enough. For a million dollars, we could build shrines to our ancestors and have plenty left over, unless Paul Revere made the family candlesticks himself. That's an extreme and rather unlikely scenario, of course, but I offer it to make a point.

Of course many of the goodies we're hoarding away in our closets have no such emotional value, and for most of those, their value is diminishing every day we keep hold of them. We may feel that it's wasteful to discard things that are still perfectly useful and that we ought to keep them because maybe we'll get more use out of them someday. But what are the odds we're really ever going to?

What the new auction culture will make clear is that we can and should generally only understand the value of what we keep by comparison to the other benefits we might accrue from those things if we could own them in another form—in cash or in kind. And as for wasting, in the auction culture, it's not the money we've spent on the things we're no longer using that we're wasting, it's the money that we could obtain by reselling them. This transition can be attributed to sweeping changes in the world of consumer goods that have dramatically impacted the way we should value our things: the cycle of innovation has reached warp speed, and durability is therefore no longer the primary source of value in so many of the things we buy.

That's why it's important to start reselling the stuff we rarely or no longer use, more often and faster.

WHAT SKIING TAUGHT ME ABOUT LIFE

Up until last year, every time I opened my hall closet, I was greeted by a pair of skis that I'd owned for more than a decade. I didn't use them anymore, and I knew that they were taking up space that could have been filled by other, more useful things. But I couldn't bring myself to get rid of them. I'm a pretty practical guy, so it's not like me to keep evidence of my irrationality around where I can see it every day.

The attachment we feel to our things is probably deeper than we tend to think, and we certainly don't think of it as wasteful. Quite the contrary. But with the advent of auction culture, it is in fact often quite wasteful. One reason this is true is that the cycle of product innovation has heated up so dramatically in recent years. The speed with which newer versions of the things we love to buy are coming to market these days is a profoundly transformative market force, and one key to changing the way we think about ownership will be to appreciate how different the cycle of product innovation is from years past. Take the case of those skis I loved so much.

Unfortunately, I wasn't one of those lucky children who are taught to ski before they can walk. My parents weren't avid sports people and they preferred spending vacations on family trips to warm destinations and cultural locales. So it wasn't until I was fifteen—teeming with adolescent pride but sensitive to the sting of humiliation—that I gathered three of my best friends, all from similar families, and we roughed the slopes without lessons, hoping to figure out the fine points of the sport by barreling down the mountain in frozen jeans. It wasn't a pretty process, and the equipment we were using wasn't helping, but we were still young enough to heal quickly, and our perseverance eventually paid off.

When I was eighteen—my fourth season skiing—I reached self-proclaimed intermediate status and rewarded myself by replacing my jeans with a one-piece ski outfit. My new duds may have made me look like a pro on the slopes, but if I took a wrong turn and found myself on an ungroomed trail, I skied (and felt) like a beginner again. It's possible that I might have given up on skiing, frustrated that I'd never become the graceful skier I wanted to be. But then I bought my first pair of parabolic skis— and learned the beauty of product innovation.

Skis are a great case in point of how the cycle of innovation has speeded up so much in recent years. When I looked into the history of skis, I was struck by just how ancient a past they have and how interesting that history is, but also by how much of the innovation in their design has happened in just the past decade or so.

The historical record is a little sketchy on the first skis and the first skiers, but it appears that men thought of strapping long boards to the bottoms of their feet as far back as ten thousand years ago, in the Stone Age, if not earlier. The vast majority of these early skis, having been made of wood, have long since rotted away, but a few have survived. In the mid-1960s, scientists working a thousand miles northeast of Moscow uncovered skis that dated back to the period from 8300 to 7000 B.C. These featured sharply upturned front ends, and one was decorated with an engraved ski head in the shape of an elk.

In case there is any doubt about how early skis were used, surviving art tells the story. According to *Ancient Inventions,* by Peter James and Nick Thorpe, "the earliest picture of a traveler using skis" turned up on the island of Rodoy in northern Norway. "Here a rock carving, fashioned around 2500 B.C., shows a figure wearing skis about twice his own length, propelling himself along with a single pole," the authors write. "Depicted in an approved skiing stance—leaning forward with knees bent—the 'Rodoy Man' seems to be wearing a costume with harelike ears, maybe to give him luck in hunting."

Developed for hunting and transportation, the basic design of skis did not change all that much over the millennia, nor did their purpose. Evidence of the recreational appeal of skiing in history is spotty. Viking king Harald Hardraade, who founded Oslo in the eleventh century, was said to enjoy racing on skis, for example. As late as 1841, the first recorded use of skis in North America, in Beloit, Wisconsin, their primary function was still practical: skis were for getting around. During the gold rush of 1849, miners heading west to the Sierra Nevada found that these "Norwegian snowshoes" were invaluable.

By 1860, however, the same miners were regularly entertaining themselves with downhill "snowshoe" races, the first recorded downhill ski races in North America. They were only a few years behind their contemporaries in Norway, who had staged the first documented ski races in 1843. Downhill skiing caught on in Europe around the same time, when an Austrian schoolteacher named Mathias Zdarsky read a book by explorer Fridtjof Nansen. The account of skiing across Greenland inspired Zdarsky to order his own pair of skis, and he later founded Europe's first ski school, in 1892, and is credited with inventing the snowplow technique.

The first important twist came in Telemark, Norway, in the mid-nineteenth century, when designers began trimming the sides of the skis, making turning easier. Austrian Rudolph Lettner invented metal-edged skis in 1928, allowing for higher speeds, and in the 1960s the Austrian firm Kneissl was among the pioneers of fiberglass ski construction. Then, from 1991 to 1992, Kneissl developed what it called the Carver Fun Ski, better known as "shaped" or "parabolic" skis. Looking almost like clown shoes, they were designed to help beginners learn to turn, but before long even expert skiers were using them. On parabolic skis, skiing is easier and less taxing on your body, you spend less time on your face, and so you look and feel better while you're on the slopes. The sport was revolutionized.

I was reading a magazine in the waiting room of my dentist's office thirteen years ago when I stumbled across an article about parabolic skis. Being the gadget addict that I am—believing that if it's the newest (and frequently most expensive), it must also be the best—I made a mental note to pick up a pair of the Elan SCX Monoblocks mentioned in the article, and bought them just as they were coming onto the market.

The technology actually worked. I flew past other people on the mountain, traversing back and forth across the snow with an ease I'd never known. It was exhilarating. I was in love with those skis. They had helped me become such a better skier that I viewed them as a symbol of my achievements. At least that's the excuse I used to justify my attachment to them long after I out-grew them. In fact, I kept them for another decade even though they hogged so much room in my closet.

.   .   .

LOVE OF A NEW technological wonder runs deep in our culture, but it was surely intensified as, during the twentieth century, the pace of innovation accelerated at unprecedented rates, bringing forth a rush of sexy new automatic and motorized devices, from radios to televisions and dishwashers to coffeemakers. They

might be commonplace now, but back then such modern con-
veniences quickly became status symbols, tangible proof of their
owners' prosperity. And at the same time, the initial impulse in-
forming the construction process was an old one—to place premi-
ums on design, workmanship, and durability. For both reasons,
manufacturers generally strove to create products that would inspire a sense of wonder that would both captivate and endure
through many long years of possession.

Let's say, for example, that you were lucky enough to be able
to go shopping for a vacuum cleaner in 1937. At that time, excel-
lence in design was somewhere between a national fad and obsession, and all the major manufacturers—General Electric, RCA,
and Westinghouse—competed with each other to find and hire
the most talented industrial designers in the world. You might
have come home with the Electrolux Model 30. It was sleek and
cylindrical, a silvery tribute to the kind of rocket ship Buck
Rogers might have piloted in the popular comic book series that
first appeared in 1928. Or, if you waited a few months, you could
have chosen the Model XXX, which came quickly behind the 30
on the Electrolux manufacturing line, commissioned by cele-
brated industrial designer Lurelle Van Arsdale Guild and built
with the lines of a Zephyr train.

Everywhere, sleek or daring new toasters and refrigerators
began popping up, with exciting names like Cubist Bold, Vulcan,
Broadway, and Novel Gothic. The 1939 Manning-Bowman Twin-
O-Matic rotating waffle iron was seen as such a magnificent device, it made its debut at the 1939 New York World's Fair.

You would have been proud of your Electrolux and your
Twin-O-Matic back then, so you would have left them out on display in corners and on countertops where your guests would no-

tice them. And you would have felt excited by the newness of the experiences they enabled. As a result, the innovations and the acquisitiveness that these devices inspired set the stage for even bigger home improvements. If appliances like vacuum cleaners or toasters came to be admired as a kind of popular art, soon shopping for a television—second only to the automobile for what it told the world about its owner—was like adding another member of the family. You expected that the unit would be around for many years, and that you (and your guests) would spend a considerable amount of time in its company.

These were exciting products, and marketers were breathless in the timbre and rhetoric of their sales pitches. "Admiral New Wonder Set!" trumpeted one magazine advertisement, featuring a wood console and ten-inch television set and depicting a row of people climbing the ramp to board an airplane. "BUILT FOR THE FUTURE," the ad proclaimed, continuing, "It's here! The wonder television receiver you have been waiting for!"

Advertisers were also savvy enough to play into the new consumer culture that innovation was inspiring. "Television sets were marketed two ways: as budget table receivers for under $200 or as sets combined with radios and phonographs in large, beautiful, expensive wood cabinets for $500," Steve Kosareff explains in *Window to the Future: The Golden Age of Television Marketing and Advertising.* "Ads targeting the wealthy who could afford the $500 sets featured formally dressed people in tuxedos and evening gowns, which sent the unmistakable message that they were better than the average, middle-class Joe who watched his $200 set (if he could afford one) in his undershirt and work pants."

The breathless tone of advertising spoke loudly to the aspirations of the public at a moment in time when it was most receptive. The combination of widespread and genuine pride in American manufacturing and its ability to meet new challenges as effectively as it had armed Allied forces to win World War II, coupled with relief about the reburgeoning of prosperity in the decades following the Great Depression, set the stage for a kind of acquisitiveness that was particularly emotional. It's no wonder that people assigned sentimental value to their new possessions. A new purchase triggered the same pride and satisfaction that I felt when I originally bought my skis.

But times have changed. Just consider the fate of the vacuum cleaner, by way of example. In 1939, the Model 30 stood proudly in living room corners across America. Forty years later, Black & Decker introduced the DustBuster, designed with completely antithetical aesthetics and for a different kind of consumer: one who prized function over form. It was meant to be lightweight and compact, to look and feel unobtrusive in use, and to be easy to store out of sight. In its first year on the market, the DustBuster sold more than a million units. By 2005, more than 150 million units had been sold worldwide.

THE SUIT WILL LAST A LIFETIME

Nineteenth-century Scottish minister William Arnot is credited with originally coining the notion that some things were made to "last a lifetime" and conceived of material durability as a reward for moral goodness: "If honor be your clothing, the suit will last a lifetime; but if clothing be your honor, it will soon be worn threadbare." This notion—the declaration of the inherent good of durable objects—was quickly taken up by early-twentieth-century manufacturers and advertisers as the key to what potential consumers would value. Accordingly, products built during the earlier part of the last century were designed and constructed, or "built to last," and the phrase became a popular sales pitch.

As innovation picked up more and more speed, eventually inventive, novel features came to take precedence over durability. Our grandparents shopped for sweaters or sofas or suitcases fully expecting that they wouldn't have to replace any of them for many, many years. Furniture was bought with the idea that if it was solidly constructed, it could be passed down from generation to generation. Even mechanical tools like typewriters were expected to last for decades, not years; the big black Underwoods and Remingtons from the 1930s and 1940s were so well made many survive today, outlasting typewriters of later design, and they have such a strong allure and identity, some people collect them.

Anyone who's ever had a new appliance die on them just after the manufacturer's warranty runs out can tell you that today durability just isn't a premium in consumer products at all anymore. There are obvious, cynical reasons to explain this evolution (or, perhaps more accurately, entropy), but manufacturers will also tell you, quite sincerely, that we're lucky to live in a time when the cycle of innovation is able to treat us to so many new, better versions of the goods that support and facilitate our lifestyles. Who wants the old model to last forever when the new one is smaller, lighter, more capable, and better looking, and has more features and provides a better experience overall?

It's this breakneck pace of innovation that has redefined what it means to squander something. Take the case of my skis again.

I bought my Elans in 1992, so they're more than fourteen years old now. That's very old for skis, though "life span" in this case is actually measured in terms of time of operation like a car or airplane engine, rather than in chronological time. The rule of thumb has always been that a quality ski has about a hundred days of use in it, although other variables factor into the equation, like the weight of the skier, how aggressively you attack the slope, and under what sort of conditions you use the ski. My Elans had about sixty days on them when I stopped using them in 1997, five years after I bought them.

Further enhancements in ski technology, including significant reductions in weight, made lugging my Elans on cross-country ski trips relatively cumbersome. So, after quite a bit of hand-wringing and a touch of remorse, I decided to leave my skis at home one trip and just brought my boots. I rented demo skis for $30 a day, came home $150 poorer for it, and skied beautifully on a pair of Volant SuperKarve I skis, which were one of that year's top models. The experiment worked so well that I barely thought about it when I set off on the next year's ski trip empty-handed.

Waiting on line to return my rentals got me thinking. My old pair of skis with state-of-the-art bindings cost me about $1,200 when I bought them five years earlier, and if I went skiing only once a year for a week or so and rented skis, they'd cost me about $200 per trip. So I could buy skis and lug them from my home to the airport to the ski resort and back, or I could rent them and—for essentially the same price—"lease" new skis on an annual basis for five or six seasons and get the best quality and design each time. I opted for the no-schlepping-and-better-equipment-for-the-same-price option and never bought another pair of skis again. But, irrationally, I kept my Elans anyway, and every time I caught a glimpse of them in my closet, I smiled.

Then, about a year ago, when I opened my closet in the attempt to get serious about uncluttering my life (New Year's resolution, just behind losing weight), I found myself staring at those Elans for a very long time. They were by far the biggest things in the closet, the most prone to tip over and knock other things down, and—practically speaking—the most useless. I realized they had to go.

"I'll sell the skis," I told my wife. And so I did, on eBay, for $100.

Had I sold the skis seven years earlier, when I actually stopped using them, I would have been able to get about $400 for them. That represents a waste to me of at least $300 in completely lost value. If you calculate the future value of what that $400 would have been worth today (based on interest rates, the return on investments, and inflation), it's probably around $800, so I'm really down about $700. That's the equivalent of opening my closet door and ritually burning a $100 bill each year as a testament to my emotional attachment to the skis.

Then we could consider the space that my skis occupied in the closet of my Manhattan apartment for the last seven years—fifteen square feet, to be exact. Rent where I live is about $5 per foot per month, or $60 per year. At fifteen square feet for seven years, I theoretically paid $420 to store a deteriorating asset. If that sounds like a ridiculous way of looking at things, consider that if I'd chosen to store the skis in the mini-storage facility down the block (where many Manhattanites house their skis in the summer), rent would have been close to double that. Without even considering the future value of my allocated rent payments, my annual ritual burning is now up to $160 every year.

FAST-FORWARD

My Elans are gone now, but I've kept the memories and associations they engendered. Not only that, but once I removed my skis from my closet, I looked at what was left with a completely fresh perspective. Instead of browsing through a collection of beloved old belongings, I suddenly saw a heap of unsold items of wasted value. And I knew with absolute certainty that I'd find the same things in any other closet I looked in. The process of realizing those things taught me a valuable lesson about how I should think about what I buy and what I keep, which I've worked hard to apply to the way I now live my life. Now I've reached a new comfort level with the auction culture way of thinking, using it to cut down on clutter while still flirting with my addiction to gadgets and new technologies . . . like the digital camera.

Probably no consumer product represents the hurried pace of innovation today versus the slower pace of yesteryear better than the digital camera.

Some 170 years ago, the Frenchman Louis-Jacques-Mandé Daguerre, a popular Parisian set designer, invented a technique for fixing a photographic image. Even in 1839, when Daguerre first made his success known, there was a public consciousness not only of the achievement it represented, but also of the future advancements it would enable. "This discovery seems like a prodigy," reported the January 7 edition of the *London Literary Gazette.* "It disconcerts all the theories of science in light and optics and, if borne out, promises to make a revolution in the arts of design."

Other methods for picture taking soon followed, notably the so-called "dry plate" process proposed in 1871 by an English doctor, Richard Leach Maddox, which involved an emulsion of gelatin and silver bromide on a glass plate. Within nine years, a halftone photograph was published in a daily newspaper, the *New York Graphic,* and twenty-four-year-old George Eastman set up his Eastman Dry Plate Company in Rochester, New York. The first Kodak camera was introduced in 1888, using paper rather than film, and a year later it was updated to use a roll of film instead of paper. The German microscope manufacturer Leitz got into the photography business in 1914, through a fellow named Oskar Barnack, who developed a camera with sprocketed 35-millimeter film, which was sold commercially as the Leica starting in 1924. New inventions and developments kept arriving steadily: Kodachrome contributed multilayered color film in 1936, and later the Japanese company Pentax developed an automatic focus mechanism and incorporated it into its cameras in the late 1950s. But the banner year was probably 1963, when Polaroid developed its first instant color film and Kodak started selling the Instamatic. This was the point at which cameras truly became a mass consumer product, purchased by working people as well as by their wealthier counterparts.

Digital imaging was developed by NASA in the 1960s for use in space probes and spy satellites, and in August 1981 Sony introduced an electronic still camera called the Mavica, which was actually a video camera that took freeze-frame images and recorded them onto a disc. The Mavica started the digital camera craze, and in 1986 Kodak developed the first megapixel sensor, which held the capacity to record 1.4 million pixels and would be developed into the modern consumer-version digital camera. However, it wasn't until 1994 that Apple introduced the QuickTake 100, which became the first digital camera to make significant inroads into the consumer market. The superiority, for general consumer purposes, of the digital camera over the old film variety is obvious. According to the Photo Marketing Association, 4.5 million digital cameras were sold in 2000, six years after the first QuickTake, compared to 19.7 million analog cameras. In five short years, that ratio has completely reversed—2005 sales figures project the sale of 4.6 million analog cameras to 20.5 million digital cameras.

As the cameras progressed, the photograph-processing business also, of course, underwent major changes. Online service providers like Shutterfly, Snapfish, and Kodak Easyshare Gallery now allow photo takers a way to access their digital images at will, store them online, and get them printed and conveniently delivered directly to their homes. Recently, inexpensive, high-quality printers were introduced that allow images to be printed at home. And these printers are now threatening yesterday's innovators like Shutterfly and its contemporaries, who are capable of becoming obsolete even faster than the conventional camera!

My father's generation thought long and hard before buying a camera, which felt like an important investment. The basic camera, once purchased, took on the feeling of a permanent possession to which you could add lenses, filters, and flashes as needed. You invested the time and energy to learn how to use it properly and expected to have it for many years. I bought myself a new camera a couple of years ago, and since then I've found out firsthand just how much has changed since my father's generation went camera shopping. . . .

I picked out a Minolta DiMAGE 7i, a then state-of-the-art digital camera with full zoom capability. It set me back $1,200, with accessories, and it had a size and shape befitting—at that time—all of the fancy technology that it contained. It was never convenient to carry around, but, oh, what a camera. The pictures it took were just incredible, and as soon as I got it home, I went snap-happy. I couldn't wait to go on a trip so I could take pictures of everything in sight, and that's just what I did.

But the snap-happy phase wore off sooner than I thought it would. Over the last two years, I've taken half a dozen major trips, and my Minolta came along with me on the first trip and the second trip and saw all kinds of action. On the third trip, it came with me, but spent all its time packed away in my suitcase. The same with my fourth trip, *and* my fifth trip. Even at home, there were times when we would be going to a party or some other special occasion and I would think about taking pictures, but my beautiful, amazing camera would always just sit in its bag because it was bulky and unwieldy and I just couldn't be bothered.

Finally my wife was fed up.

"We miss all these opportunities to take pictures," she told me. "Let's just buy a portable little camera that I can put in my purse."

I did what any smart husband would do. I went out and bought us a new camera. As soon as I got to the store and started learning about all the new features, it wasn't difficult to discover genuine enthusiasm. I picked out a Sony T1, just as state-of-the-art as the DiMAGE was when I bought it, and a fraction of the size. The Sony T1 set me back $500 and has the same 5-megapixel resolution, which is excellent, but it is such a thin little nothing, I can carry it in my pocket and hardly even know it's there. My wife and I both love the camera, and now when we go on a weekend getaway, to a birthday party or a baby shower or even just out with friends, we can snap a few pictures and have a way to remember the day.

My Minolta was, of course, taking up space in the same closet my Elans had, but the situations didn't feel comparable. I knew I'd never use my parabolic skis again and I couldn't say the same about the camera. So I tried to determine—analytically—what kind of value the Minolta retained, at least according to the market. I decided to consult eBay, where a lot of identical cameras were up for sale. Though a small part of me took comfort in the evidence that mine was a shared dilemma, with so many cameras on the market, my $1,200 model was only going to sell for about $350. From a value standpoint, I felt like I was getting ripped off. But from an economic standpoint, it didn't matter what *I* thought the camera was worth. From an economic standpoint, things are only worth what other people will pay for them.

"Why don't I just keep it?" I thought to myself. "So I won't use it every day. But I'll have it the next time I go on a safari."

Then it dawned on me: if, in two or three years down the road, I am able to go on a safari, or visit some beautiful, distant locale that would beg to be captured by a fancy, bulky, professional-looking camera that takes gorgeous, high-quality pictures, I can always buy a Minolta DiMAGE 7i back from someone else. As sure as I am about the value being $350 today, I'm just as certain that it's going to be less than that tomorrow—a lot less. So I would win both ways; I'd make some money now and pay less later.

I decided to sell my Minolta and I felt good about it . . . just up until the point when I realized that if I had embraced this kind of thinking a year or two earlier when I actually stopped using the camera, I probably would have gotten another few hundred dollars for it. I could, essentially, have traded it for my Sony—the camera that's right for me right now. It was suddenly boldly clear that to keep it idle in my closet while its value continued to decline was simply actually wasteful.

THE ECONOMICS OF LETTING GO

Instead of worrying or regretting that I'm squandering my investment in things that I expected to get more use from—like my Elans and Minolta—I now celebrate the fact that I have the opportunity to trade in so many things I've bought to get new things that I want more. My grandfather, who always exhorted me to clean my dinner plate, certainly would have shaken his head at the piles of things that I've turned over while they still had "a few good wearings in them," but he didn't know a world where there were better cuts of skis and smaller digital chips available every few months. I'm not losing when I put my "like new" Minolta on the closet shelf, or—for that matter—on eBay's block; I'm benefiting from a situation—a rush—that my parents and grandparents never knew.

It's generally taken a milestone event to get many of us to release the stranglehold with which we cling to our possessions. These catalysts—the D events: death, divorce, debt, downsizing— are generally unpleasant, but the stripping down (or parsing out) that they require can have a salutary effect.

The problem is, from an economic standpoint, that by the time these events usually occur—late, or at least later, in life—the value of many of our possessions has dwindled, often to nothing. It's easy to believe that this depreciation is painless, since it occurs over many years. But that's not exactly true, and once we learn to look at the residual value that we're losing, starting from the moment that it begins to wane, we see why.

Though we have now lived in relatively prosperous times for decades, and rapid advances in technology have occurred for many years, our behavior still hasn't changed fundamentally because we haven't changed our understanding of the concept of value. What, we must ask ourselves, is the alternative? Because—unlike many of our predecessors—with the advent of auction culture, we do have a good alternative.

If we could remove irrational sentiment from the equation entirely, we would behave in an absolutely economically sound manner, meaning that if we could analyze the true depreciation curve of an item, including its actual value and the costs associated with selling it, we could point to the exact location on the curve just before the steepest decline in value, which would signify the most appropriate time to sell, and seize that as the moment to replace our old assets with the new, better versions. I propose that, in the future, this is exactly what will happen, because the opportunity to take the plunge into the auction culture will be ubiquitous and the incentive will be irresistible.

The transition from our accumulation nation to that of the auction culture promises substantial rewards, not just for the individuals who earn money by reselling their used goods, but for society as a whole. Far from encouraging waste, the auction culture will actually discourage waste as it helps us maximize the true value of our possessions.

One of the most famous concepts of economics is Adam Smith's theory of the "invisible hand," the notion that when individuals act to further their own self-interests, society as a whole benefits. Correspondingly, when individuals behave inefficiently, society suffers for it. As Smith put it, "The annual revenue of every society is always precisely equal to the exchangeable value of the whole annual produce of its industry, or rather is precisely the same thing with that exchangeable value."

Exchangeable value. Even in Smith's day, when the durability of things was prized, he realized that wealth could be created in the exchange of things—the exchange of things *from* those for whom they held less value *to* those for whom they would be a boon. That's the concept we need to internalize.

In our failure to act efficiently, the big loser has been society. And the amount lost can be measured in the trillions. According to an ACNielsen report issued in October 2004, American households have accumulated an average of more than $2,200 in goods they no longer use, which retain a market value of nearly half that. With more than 110 million households in the United States, that works out to an aggregate of more than $250 billion in lost value already and another $250 billion that will, likewise, soon dwindle to nothing if things don't change. This number grows every day. And our story is repeated in every developed nation in the world.

But fortunately, auction culture is evolving to shed light on the true value of every item up for sale. This clarity will fundamentally redefine our relationships with the things we own. We won't actually need to play with depreciation curves or keep value charts for our possessions (though I guarantee that some of us will significantly improve our lives doing just that); we'll just need to be open to experimenting with a new lifestyle—and let the benefits of more modern behavior speak for themselves.

2 SECONDHAND NATION
Minding the Liquidity Gap

Simon Foster was a man who just needed money to pay the rent. He was unemployed, with few prospects and an empty bank account, forced to resort to a last-ditch option. He made for his local pawnshop to sell some personal items, but it turned out that the proprietor didn't want any of his stuff. Instead, he told Foster he would let him pawn some of his memories. Surprised, confused, but without alternatives, Foster agreed, and quickly learned that there was a decent market for memories of first kisses, birthdays, and graduations. Foster walked away with good money that day. Soon, though, he realized that he needed his memories back in order to get a new job. He returned to the pawnshop, this time with a gun, and demanded that the owner return what he felt was rightfully his. The proprietor complied, handing over the memories. But that day, Simon

Foster got a lot more than he bargained for. The shopkeeper gave him back more that just his own memories—he got other people's memories as well.

Fans of the classic television series *The Twilight Zone* might recognize Simon Foster as a character from one of its episodes. Viewers of the show got an opportunity to watch the inefficiencies of a fantasy secondhand market in memories by imagining a world where you can pawn them like used musical instruments.

The accumulation mentality only goes so far in explaining our hoarding behavior. The aversion we have towards reselling our possessions also comes from the nature of the secondhand-goods markets themselves: unsavory and stigmatized at one end, elitist and inaccessible at the other, and inefficient all the way through. Historically, when it actually came time to sell something, the options for doing so were so limited and inefficient that we usually just shrugged and let the sleeping boxes lie. EBay has made buying and selling used goods a whole lot sexier, but still not mainstream. So why will that change? The underlying economic reason that the auction culture will become so mainstream in the future is that, unlike all the traditional secondary-goods markets, the online exchanges of the evolving auction culture will one day soon offer almost perfect liquidity.

This is, at heart, why online auction sites have been so revolutionary—they are the first relatively efficient, and increasingly liquid, marketplaces for the exchange of previously owned goods. They have begun to allow us—finally—to extract "fair value" for our used stuff, and now they're becoming remarkably convenient as well. A quick history of the prior alternatives reveals just how far we've come, especially when you take into account how old these marketplaces are and the limitations inherent in all of them. It also reveals the gaping hole in the marketplace for secondary goods that auction culture is filling faster than you can say "Sold!"

GOT JUNK?

Starting at the bottom of the barrel, there has long been a market for goods that most people would consider outright junk.

Centuries ago, most cultures had some version of a junk dealer similar to what in England was called the "ragman." He wheeled a cart through poor neighborhoods, calling out "Any old iron!" and "Rag and bone!" He purchased other people's discards for pennies and would enhance the items before reselling them. He would move from one neighborhood to the next, where children clamored to be first in line to pet the horse. The term "ragman" dates back far enough that a popular seventeenth-century English song called "Joan's Ale" devotes a few lines to him:

The Rag Man being weary with the burden he did carry
He swore he would be merry and spend a shilling or two.
He told his hostess to her face the chimney-corner was his place
And he began to drink apace whilst Joan's ale was new.

Junk collectors have persisted through the years and all around the world. In Israel, for example, junk dealers are famous for roaming the streets and calling out, *"Alte zakhen,"* Yiddish for "old things." The term has a long history among Israeli Arabs and Arabs in the Palestinian territories, according to a 2001 article in the Yiddish newspaper the *Forward*. The author remembers hearing the dealers when he first settled in Israel thirty years ago. "Then as now, a beat-up pick-up truck would occasionally cruise through the neighborhood and an Arabic-accented voice would blare, whether unassisted or via a loudspeaker, '*A-a-lte za-KHEN, a-a-lte za-KHEN.*' The owner of the truck, generally a Palestinian from the West Bank, was not selling but buying—old clothes, old mattresses, broken furniture, busted appliances, anything in the attic or storeroom that might be fixed and resold in an Arab village."

Today, the largest junk-removal service in North America is 1-800-GOT-JUNK. Its founder, Brian Scudamore, started the company in 1989 with $700, a truck, and help from a buddy. They called themselves Rubbish Boys. Now, for a fee, the company will send its employees to your home at your convenience. They'll accept any nonhazardous material you don't want that two people can lift, and they'll haul it to a landfill or transfer station, or just recycle it.

The rag trade is credited with giving birth to the ever more popular flea market. In France, the ragman had a counterpart known as a *biffin* or *chiffonier.* But the traveling ragmen fell under attack in France following a cholera outbreak in 1832. Since it was their practice to accumulate discarded objects for resale, the risk of infection ran high. Markets were also banned in Paris over cholera fears. But the *biffins* figured out a way to keep selling. According to the association of the Paris Saint-Ouen flea markets, the exiled sellers teamed up with bric-a-brac traders and established the first flea market—literally *marché aux puces,* or "market of fleas"—just outside the city walls in Saint-Ouen, beyond the ban's reach. There are conflicting stories about exactly how the flea market got its name, but in all likelihood it came from the fleas that initially infested furniture and clothing being peddled.

Because selling goods at the flea market required attending your stall all day, sellers gathered a significant number of goods to display for sale. The concentration of goods for sale in turn attracted more and more buyers and the markets became hugely popular. As Albert LaFarge notes in his *U.S. Flea Market Directory,* "Today's American flea market is a modern version of a phenomenon that has endured throughout history in all civilized societies—wherever there is a high concentration of people, there will be market days when they assemble for the exchange of goods and services."

CLEAN SWEEP

The more intimate version of a flea market is, of course, the yard sale. Whatever you call them in your neighborhood—yard sales, garage sales, or rummage sales—they're all predominantly American phenomena that took off in suburbia during the late 1960s and early 1970s. The funny thing about those scraps you have tucked away in your basements, attics, and the scary corners of your closets is that there's usually someone who will get up extremely early and drive over to your home just to be first to see them on sale.

In 1967, the *Los Angeles Times* breathlessly described the garage sale as part community event, part gamble. "A family can always get eating money," one garage sale organizer told *L.A. Times* reporter Donna Schiebe. "Somewhere in every household there's something someone else wants more than you do." That's why yard sales can be a great way to make some quick cash, but they are not the most effective way to get the highest value for your possessions, not by a long shot. Even with modern helpers like online garage sale listing services, a sale still takes at least a day to organize and run, if not an entire weekend. The desire to just get rid of your things fast also means that you make relatively little profit. You're willing to take a lower price just so you don't have to put all that stuff back in storage or drive it over to the thrift store. Furthermore, it's unlikely that you'll draw in the largest customer base possible. People will find you by word of mouth, through primitive signs, and by driving down your street. Ultimately, you are limited to a very local base of potential customers.

Speaking of taking a low price, of all the channels to the secondary market, none is as onerous to the seller as the pawnshop, an institution as old as antiquity itself. By definition, someone ducking into a pawnshop to raise some quick cash is in no position to hold out for fair value. Someone desperate for money can bring something valuable, like a watch or musical instrument, to a pawnbroker as collateral for a loan equal to a percentage of the item's value. If the seller doesn't repay the obligation within an agreed-upon amount of time, the pawnbroker reserves the right to sell the collateral as a way to recoup the loan. Since nearly 20 percent of all pawned items are never reclaimed by their owners, actual value is heavily discounted, and "loans" are transacted at seemingly usurious rates to protect the shopkeeper. A silver candelabra becomes a month's rent money, or the Rolex watch you love helps cover the next several car payments. Pawnshops are generally used only by those with no alternative and may seem like an anachronism, but in fact their numbers grew steadily throughout the twentieth century, and a big upswing in the 1980s brought the total number in the United States to 14,000 by 1995, or one for every 17,900 people, according to the National Pawnbrokers Association.

YOUR POSSESSIONS "IN PRINT"

A better option for selling things of any real value is through classified advertising, which also has a long history. Classified ads have been a staple of newspapers dating back centuries. London newspapers, for example, started to run classified advertising in the 1640s.

Classifieds offer a higher degree of liquidity. After all, you reach more eyeballs listing a classified ad in a paper that has a circulation in the thousands than a lone handwritten sign taped to a tree near your home. The more potential customers who see your listing, the greater the likelihood that you'll be able to sell your used stuff for a higher price. But even with expansive circulations, using the classifieds to advertise personal possessions still limits you to your local market.

Beyond the limited scope of circulation, classified ads have other drawbacks. One of the burdens of a classified ad that you might not consider before placing one is that you have to deal with the public. You are, in essence, advertising your personal information. You're putting your telephone number into the public sphere so that anybody can communicate with you. Then you have to actually talk to a stranger, and as commonplace as that might sound, it can be a very invasive experience for people who are not used to it or try to avoid it. My parents bought and sold old sets of encyclopedias that way. Today, I would not feel comfortable having a complete stranger come into my apartment to peruse my library if I decided to sell a set of encyclopedias.

If the thought of someone pawing your books is unnerving, cars can make the classified ad experience even more awkward. My first car was a bright red 1983 Toyota Celica GTS, which my parents purchased for me my freshman year of college. Three weeks after I drove it off the lot, someone stole it—college papers, backpack, and all. The insurance money paid for my ability to buy a silver Volkswagen Scirocco, California Edition, which I sold to my younger brother several years later. When I found an advertisement for a used red Nissan 300ZX Turbo in excellent condition for around $12,000, I made a trip to a home remotely located in the Hollywood Hills. It wasn't exactly the safest feeling being in some stranger's backyard in the middle of nowhere to buy a car, but it turned out to be a smart move. A year and a half later, I resold the car for $14,000, a $2,000 profit. Of course, in order for that to happen, a bunch of strangers had to come and test-drive *my* car. It's the last time I put myself in that situation and have always opted to trade in my cars ever since.

RENTING SPACE IN A STORE

While classified ads require the seller to do the legwork, venues such as antique shops and consignment stores give the seller a break in exchange for control over the sales process.

Consignment shops are a special category all their own in the United States, making up part of what the National Association of Resale & Thrift Shops calls a multibillion-dollar resale industry. These stores generate a limited but acceptable form of liquidity, providing sellers a discreet way to get rid of their goods by targeting interested customers. At consignment shops, the store manager decides on a price, tags the items, puts them on display, and reduces the price every month until they sell. On average, the display lasts from one to three months, and when the merchandise sells, the store pays you an agreed-upon percentage. Most pay between 40 and 60 percent of the selling price and are selective in what they accept.

For all their discretion and potential, consignment stores still have significant limitations. The shopkeeper may set the price too low, and it can take a long time to get your cash. Another downside is that your expensive clothing that hasn't seen the light of day in more than a year may not be accepted because it isn't expensive enough for the shop. And these stores also offer only limited, local exposure for your goods. The Gucci handbag that you paid $800 for three years ago but no longer use will get you only $50 because there just aren't enough people shopping the store to create the necessary demand. Many local consignment shops also limit their merchandise to a specific category like clothing, furniture, or collectibles.

SERIOUS VALUE

Of all the traditional secondary marketplaces, the auction house has offered the most liquidity by far. Auction houses have done brisk business over the years without the stigma associated with the other venues that sell used goods. Today auction houses facilitate both high-brow affairs open only to attract a precious, glittering few as well as more commercial events that are accessible to the general public.

Marlon Brando's final days on Earth bordered on the kind of madness he had so artfully brought to life in his eerie role in the film *Apocalypse Now*. His biographer, Peter Manso, wrote that the actor had holed himself up in his bedroom while his house became infested with rodents. Manso added that Brando's longtime business manager began getting odd messages from the star, including one asking her to make it seem as though he didn't live in California so he wouldn't have to pay taxes. Another note, according to Manso, requested that Brando's bedroom be sealed and padlocked after his death. "They will steal the buttons off my shirt," he wrote.

Actually, they'd buy them. . . . More than 250 of the late star's belongings went on Christie's auction block in 2005. Everything from Brando's annotated copy of the *Godfather* script to a pair of Cuban bongo drums was cataloged, valued, and ready for eager bidders. Weeks before the auction was scheduled to start in New York, the public had a chance to go see the collection. Christie's hosted film screenings and even a panel discussion about Brando, all in the name of getting the most value out of the star's bric-a-brac. Finally, at noon on June 30, 2005, the auction got under way. Five hundred spectators and bidders packed Christie's New York showroom to watch more than 250 lots go on the block, according to ArtDaily.com. Brando enthusiasts from all over the world bid in absentia in a variety of ways, but notably not via e-mail.

Auction houses like Christie's have long based their success on reaching the right buyers. The faster they sell and the more money they fetch, the more liquid the system and the more likely people are to use it. The six-and-a-half-hour Personal Property of Marlon Brando auction at Christie's raked in nearly $2.4 million, including $312,800 for the script and $11,000 for the set of bongos. But other items sold in the low hundreds, making pieces of Brando accessible to the masses.

While flea markets, pawnbrokers, and consignment stores all have had various social stigmas associated with them, with the auction house the reverse is true. Fine auction houses have long been the vehicles of the rich, and have succeeded in creating an environment so redolent of privilege that it is not only socially acceptable for the elite to sell and buy through this channel, it has actually been considered posh.

The auction houses not only have no stigma, but they've perfected the art of driving up prices, harnessing the enormous economic power of competitive bidding, which is so vital to the liquidity offered by the new online exchanges. Auctions actually date back to volatile ancient Rome, where the Praetorian Guard infamously put the entire Roman Empire up for bid in 193 AD. The English word "auction" actually comes from the Latin *augere,* which means to increase or augment. An auction's lucrative potential became apparent early on to a London bookseller named Samuel Baker in the eighteenth century. Baker had on his hands a personal library of 457 volumes that had belonged to the late Right Honorable Sir John Stanley. He didn't quite know what to do with the diverse collection "containing several hundred scarce and valuable books in all branches of Polite Literature." Baker decided to hold an auction, and on March 11, 1744, he sold the books for a handsome profit of a few hundred pounds. Baker eventually transformed the business into an exclusive auction house for books. After Baker died, in 1778, the business ultimately landed with the family of his nephew, John Sotheby, who established the firm's lofty reputation by maintaining Baker's emphasis on book auctions.

While Sotheby's thrived, former naval officer James Christie the Elder was busy establishing a competing auction house in 1766 in London. Even though the first sale included chamber pots, Christie cultivated friendships with leading artists of his day, and his auction house soon became a gathering place for dealers and collectors. Christie's made its name with a number of high-profile events soon after opening, including the 1778 sale of Sir Horace Walpole's art collection to Catherine the Great, who needed pictures to fill the Hermitage in St. Petersburg. When Madame du Barry, Louis XV's mistress, went to the guillotine in France during the French Revolution, Christie's managed the 1795 sale of her jewels. Nearly two decades later, Christie's opened a sale room in New York City, where it would one day sell Van Gogh's melancholy *Portrait of Dr. Gachet* for a record $82.5 million. Auctions have always been a great way to get the highest price possible—even seemingly irrational prices—for previously owned goods.

The big problem with auction houses, of course, is that they are limited to a small group of people who can afford to either provide the items for sale or bid on them. Even though high-end auction houses have become more accessible to the public in recent years, there are still limits to liquidity there. Specialized auctions need time and effort to organize, as well as a critical mass of similar or related objects to attract the right group of potential buyers. Generally, you can't count on an auction house to satisfy an immediate or specific need. If you want Christie's or Sotheby's to take your feather-filled golf ball from a bygone sports era, for example, you'll have to wait until it fits into a collection, just like you will if you're a prospective bidder looking for an ancient feather-filled golf ball. The golf ball must also be valuable enough in their eyes to be worthy of their venue.

When the auction platform is maximized, it is the channel most capable of generating fair market value, and that power of the auction to generate value is fundamental to the boom in liquidity we'll see in the new auction culture. The other marketplaces can hardly reach the auction system's potential. For a graphic representation of the historic secondary market channels relative to each other, consider the chart below:

Historic Secondary-Market Channels

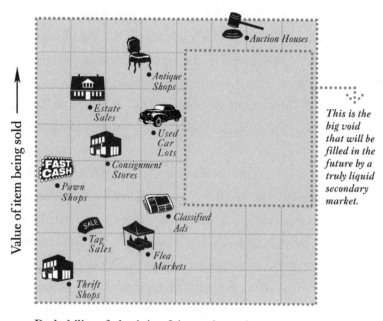

This is the big void that will be filled in the future by a truly liquid secondary market.

Value of item being sold →

Probability of obtaining fair market value →

The more you move to the right in the chart, the more liquid the market is. The more you move up, the more valuable the items are that traditionally sell in the respective venue. In the top right corner you have the auction houses, which stand apart from all other categories. Used car lots and classified ads both do relatively well in terms of providing some liquidity. Couched between classified ads and auction houses, however, there is a huge void where the items of medium-range value ought to be bought and sold. And yet, for the most part, nobody caters to that area today. As truly liquid secondary markets evolve, this void will be filled.

THE CAR MARKET: A SIGN OF THINGS TO COME

The market for used cars allows us to preview what the void will look like when it is filled in the near future. It is the closest market to resemble how and why the secondary-goods marketplace will evolve with the massive adoption of online auction reselling. Many of the innovations to come to the world of online exchanges can be found in the history of how the used-car market developed.

The cheaply built Model T that rolled out of Henry Ford's Piquette plant in Detroit in 1908 was an instant hit with wealthy and working-class people alike. Everyone wanted one. Even though the car was reliable, it took a while for Ford to produce a second model. A small and uncertain secondary market in Model Ts began to develop in the meantime. The automobile was such a wonder, so expensive, and so large that its owners couldn't just forget they owned one, like they could with a pair of suspenders or a box of old shoes. When Ford launched an automotive revolution, he helped launch the used-car business, too. In fact, when Ford had moved technologically past the first "horseless carriage" he built in 1896, he sold it for $200 to a man named Charles Ainsley, who later sold it to a bicycle dealer. When it came to personal transportation, there was a use for anything that worked.

The automobile had a unique impact on the secondary market for two reasons: the size of the car itself, and the size of the investment it required. In the automobile's early days, it was such a coveted possession that Ford was four months behind in production before his new assembly line opened in 1913. Nevertheless, it became clear that many of his customers could just barely front the money to purchase one of the new vehicles; they could manage to pay it off eventually, but it was a large investment. The car was so important that people who bought one had to plan accordingly, adjusting their food budgets in order to make payments. Before the Model T, possessions that involved that kind of financial planning included items like pianos and sewing machines. After World War I, dealers introduced the installment payment plan so that the average American had an easier time owning a car.

Few people who wanted a new car could afford to let their old one rust on the back lawn. The automobile was simply too expensive to waste. Limited storage space for them further discouraged the hoarding instinct—you couldn't really take it apart to store in the basement. In addition, there were plenty of people who couldn't afford new ones but who were perfectly happy to get all the mileage they could out of a used one. When old Model Ts began to wear out by the 1920s, buyers brought them back to dealers for down payments on the latest model, leading to a new trade business.

A man named Les Kelley then made it even easier to buy and sell secondhand cars. A preacher's son from Arkansas, Kelley had been broke when he moved to Los Angeles in 1914. Soon, however, he and his brother began earning money by repairing and reselling old Model Ts. It took only a few repairs to get going. The Kelley Kar Company grew steadily into the largest automobile dealership in the world.

Kelley developed a reputation among car dealers for his skill in assessing a car's value. He was always on the lookout for used cars to turn around, and he got into the habit of putting together a list of different car makes and how much he would pay to buy them for refurbishment. Kelley circulated this list to banks and other dealers so that they could know what cars he was looking for and what he was willing to pay for them. Soon prospective car buyers were asking to consult his list to see how much their used cars were worth. Kelley had an idea: why not publish the list and charge for it? From there, it didn't take long until Kelley released the first *Blue Book of Motor Car Values,* in 1926.

Kelley wasn't the only one to recognize the new kinds of opportunities that the booming business in automobiles could create for a knowledgeable and enterprising vendor. A Philadelphia dealer named Martin H. Bury published his own booklet in 1938, which he sold for twenty-five cents per copy of forty-four pages containing detailed, practical information about making sound decisions when buying a used car. Buy from a reputable dealer with service facilities, Bury advised. Buy in the winter—prices are lower and good winter cars are usually better summer cars. Buy standard makes. Beware of worn upholstery, he warned, because the innards may be worse. More advice from Bury: don't believe speedometer mileage, look at the pedal wear, and a new paint job sometimes covers a multitude of sins. These were actually incredibly helpful bits of wisdom for aspiring buyers unfamiliar with the process of purchasing a used car.

But in terms of articulating specific, practical information about valuing cars by their make and model over time, Les Kelley remained the standard-bearer. That first *Blue Book of Motor Car Values* gave the factory list price and present-day cash value of thousands of cars, from Pierce-Arrows to Hupmobiles and Duesenbergs to Cadillacs (in 1926, a Packard sedan limousine was worth as much as $3,825, but a 1921 Nash was lucky to get $50). The book helped Kelley build a massive following, and it became so popular that Kelley eventually phased out of the used-car business to focus on the *Blue Book*.

Though Kelley's *Blue Book* fueled the growth of the used-car business, it had a much more profound impact on the way buyers purchased new cars. The *Blue Book* gave buyers an idea of what their car would be worth in the future. All they had to do was take a look at how well the car make in a similar model was doing a few years out. That key piece of information enabled buyers to estimate the cost of owning a car over a certain period of time. And knowing the approximate value of what the car would fetch in the secondary market gave people the confidence to buy it in the primary market.

Then, during World War II, the used-car business exploded. Automobile factories had stopped making civilian vehicles altogether to join the war effort, forcing a large segment of the population to refurbish the cars they owned or start buying used ones. It became universally acceptable to sell and buy previously owned vehicles regardless of your socioeconomic standing. When the car production kick started again after the war, it no longer mattered if you were rich or poor—you sold your car when you decided to get a new one.

When the war caused a surge in demand for used cars, a group of men in Pennsylvania decided to capitalize on it with their own particular take. In 1945, Jake Ruhl, Paul Stern, B. Z. Mellinger, and Art Walters founded Manheim Auto Auction in Manheim, Pennsylvania. Their first sale turned over only three cars, but they kept at it and succeeded wildly. The auction format worked in their favor as the growing circle of serious bidders brought the price closer and closer to fair value for the vehicles. Banks, financing companies, and even manufacturers with slightly used cars turned to Manheim Auto Auctions as an easy way to unload the cars. By 1959, the Manheim Auto Auction had become the largest auto auction in the world. Manheim created large lots throughout the country, building up inventory through purchases from insurance companies, dealers, and rental car companies. Manheim was an early presence on the Web, too, establishing AutoTrader.com in 1996.

The used-car market became increasingly liquid throughout the 1980s, when more families considered adding a second car. They turned increasingly to used-car lots, where most used cars were still paid for in cash. At that time, leases were rare and when they were arranged it was only for the occasional professional or business. For everyone else, financing a new car usually meant lining up a loan. When changes in the tax law made car loans less attractive and the price of new cars began to spike, however, buyers looked for a new option. In an echo of the automobile's early days, manufacturers started partnering with finance companies to make it easier for prospective buyers to drive off in their dream cars. They began offering leases. Lessees simply paid to use the cars for a few years, and then brought the car back. With a "closed-end" lease, also known as a "walk-away" lease, you could walk away as soon as the lease was over. The risk of ownership stays with the leasing company, and if the car depreciates more than they were estimating, you still don't owe a penny.

Leasing introduced the revolutionary concept of temporary ownership to buyers, as well as the prospect of "reaching" for vehicles that were too expensive to own but affordable to lease.

We'll see both concepts, as well as the related practice of "trading up" at play in a big way as the auction culture develops.

Leasing made economic sense for the car dealerships, too. Dealers were, in essence, selling the temporary ownership of a car for a price equal to the difference between the purchase price on day one and the estimated residual value at a certain point in the future, plus interest. Soon dealerships directed their salespeople to encourage leasing. The number of new-car customers opting to lease, rather than own, increased from a tiny percentage to fully one-third of all new cars, trucks, vans, and SUVs.

At the same time as leasing picked up in popularity, improvements in manufacturing quality throughout the 1980s and 1990s translated into cars that lasted longer. You could buy a new car and reasonably expect it to last you a full ten years or more. This also meant that the value of your car didn't depreciate as dramatically as it once did—at least, once you got past the big drop in price the minute you drove the car away from the dealership. Cars that maintained greater relative value a few years after purchase were especially attractive to lessees, since monthly lease payments would be based on the finance company's estimate of what the car would be worth at auction at the end of the lease. Accordingly, your monthly payments would be less for a car that maintained a higher residual value than for one that depreciated more quickly.

Soon the market became flooded with two- and three-year-old cars that were only 20 or 30 percent along in their expected life spans. These were nothing like the lemons in the old-fashioned stereotype—boxy clunkers sold by fast-talking disreputable men with slicked-back hair, polyester jackets, and fake grins. Instead, these were solidly made, well-maintained vehicles that could be called "almost new" without a wink or a nudge. And every year the car companies rolled out more of them. At the same time, the car market began evolving into a more competitive industry as manufacturers and dealers fought ferociously to win over clients. This caused the dealerships in particular to feel a squeeze on their profits. Many dealers found that by entering the burgeoning used-car market as an adjunct to their core business, they could supplement the lost income.

Trade-ins and trade-ups have become so pervasive in the car market that it's become the norm to view an automobile as a temporary asset. As the auction culture goes more and more mainstream, we'll see these same key changes in the market for many goods. In the near future, we will evolve into a society that is programmed to view the ownership of most things as temporary—just like our perception of cars today. As the secondary market gets more liquid, more and more products will actually be available on a leasing basis in a manner very similar to the way cars are acquired today. To stay in the game, manufacturers will be forced to "build to last" again in response to a base of consumers who will demand to lease only higher quality and more durable goods that retain value.

Before that can happen, of course, a number of improvements must be made in the online exchanges. The evolution of the secondary market will inevitably be driven largely by eBay. The fact is that eBay is the newest entrant and top rung on the ladder of new secondary-market channels. But while eBay has reinvented the way people buy and sell, its true significance to society currently rests on whether it can eventually fulfill its promise of being the most efficient way to that truly liquid marketplace the online auction mechanism has the potential to deliver.

3 AUCTION FEVER
Catalyst for a Cultural Revolution

One of the great lessons of eBay has been: never underestimate the value that something you couldn't care less about might have for someone else, maybe even for a vast network of enthusiasts who will bid like crazy for it.

Vienna businessman Eduard Haas III was a cigarette smoker, so he knew how hard it was to quit. He was already a wealthy man thanks to success with a baking powder and cake mix business, when it occurred to him that one way to distract hard-core smokers from their cravings might be to encourage them to keep their mouths full and their taste buds busy with something else. In 1927, he invented the Nicorette of his day, a small, brick-shaped, strongly flavored mint made by dropping peppermint oil onto a tablet of compressed sugar. This was the world's first breath mint, and Haas gave it a pleasingly simple name derived from the German word for peppermint, *Pfeffer-minz*. PEZ, the contraction Haas chose, was short, snappy, and memorable. He used a metal container designed to look like a Bic lighter as packaging.

"Eat a peppermint instead," the early PEZ ads urged smokers.

Tins of the little rectangular mints were enough of a hit in Austria that Haas started exporting them to the United States in 1952, packaging them inside toy guns. Americans were slow to embrace PEZ, so five years later, armed with extensive market research, the company decided to try putting the mints in plastic dispensers shaped like animals. Pulling the figurine head back pushed the candy out, a gimmick designed to appeal to children, as was the introduction of fruit-flavored varieties. This new version of the candy sold well, but much more interesting is the fact that a mass phenomenon developed as generations of children grew up fascinated with PEZ dispensers. As the variety of plastic curiosities extended into the hundreds—everything from angels to zebras—the item became a popular collectible.

Collectors are, by nature, active participants in the second-hand goods market since much of what they seek to acquire for their collections has already been owned by someone else. So it's not surprising that collectors of PEZ dispensers and similar novelties helped spur eBay's initial expansion. Collector groups formed communities and discussions around their favorite things and brought the treasure hunt feel of rummaging through yard sales to the Internet. EBay helped them discover that *one* dispenser they'd been looking for forever. The unprecedented ability for people to trade with strangers living in another part of the country, and eventually all over the world, and to communicate with a like-minded community was the driving force that made eBay one of the huge successes of the dot-com boom.

EBay's phenomenal growth is now legendary, but it's instructive to visit some of the facts and figures as the company reached new benchmarks. In early 2000, five years into its existence, eBay's CEO Meg Whitman sent a letter to stockholders reporting what an amazing year it had been for the company. She also wanted to give them some perspective on how much it had grown. In January 1999, eBay had 2.2 million registered users, she said, comparing the number of users to the population of Portland, Oregon. By the year's end, the number had risen almost five times, to 10 million people. That, Whitman wrote, equaled the size of the population of the entire state of Michigan.

Today, eBay's business is better than good. It's unbelievable. The global user community has grown to more than 150 million people, equivalent to more than half the entire U.S. population. And the company had a watershed year in 2004, when $34.2 billion in goods were sold on its site, enough activity to make eBay the eleventh-largest retailer in the United States, just below national giants like Wal-Mart, Home Depot, and Kmart.

There are many keys to eBay's success, but the overall explanation comes down to the organic way in which eBay evolved to serve a community of users and, crucially important, to offer them liquidity in both buying and selling such a vast offering of used goods. If you know the story of eBay's founding and evolution, you may want to skip the account below and jump ahead to page 69. (Not Just for the Mavens Anymore), but for those who don't know the story, it's one of the great business triumphs of our time, and it speaks volumes about why auction culture is here to stay.

A VIRAL REVOLUTION

It turns out that one of those zealous PEZ collectors mentioned above ultimately played an unexpected role in eBay's history.

Many news stories about eBay's beginnings still repeat the tale that starts with one particular dinner eBay founder Pierre Omidyar was sharing with his fiancée, Pam Wesley, at home in Campbell, California, when the conversation turned to PEZ. Wesley loved to collect the dispensers. When she moved from Boston to California, Wesley didn't know other people who shared her passion for PEZ dispensers. Searching for a way to help, Omidyar created eBay so Wesley could connect to other PEZ collectors.

How sweet a story, and yet, how false.

The truth is more complicated than the PEZ story, which was concocted by eBay's first full-time employee, Mary Lou Song, to bring media attention to the company, according to Adam Cohen's book *The Perfect Store: Inside eBay.* Wesley did like PEZ dispensers, but Omidyar was thinking more about code than candy when he came up with eBay's original site, Auction-Web. In the Internet's early days, when logging online usually meant enduring the screechy multipitched dial-up sound of a modem, Omidyar was an idealistic computer scientist with a ponytail and a scruffy goatee who hoped to change the secondary marketplace. He saw companies begin to strategize ways to move their businesses online and sell more things to more people. Omidyar was working at a mobile communications start-up in Silicon Valley with a slew of ex-Apple employees when he decided to transfer control of commerce away from companies and into the hands of individuals. His libertarian take on capitalism inspired him to spend Labor Day weekend 1995 working on the project that would later pull more than 150 million people into a new economic world.

AuctionWeb began as a hobby for Omidyar, a program he cobbled together using free software available online. He wasn't out to make money. His goal was to create a marketplace where everyone was on equal footing and, in his mind, the auction format was the only one that could do that, he told *Forbes* in 2005.

Omidyar simply added AuctionWeb to his personal site, Echo Bay Technology Group, a name he plucked out of the air because he liked how it sounded, according to Cohen's book. When he had initially tried to register echobay.com, it was already claimed, so he had to come up with something else. He went with the simplest abbreviation, eBay.com. The primitive site did say "AuctionWeb" in plain typeface on a gray background, but no one paid much attention to that. As more people heard about AuctionWeb and visited Omidyar's personal site, they started referring to AuctionWeb as "eBay"—the letters they had to type into their Internet browser.

The early version of eBay let users list items, view items, and place bids. And it was free. Traffic built slowly as Omidyar spread the word about his site through Usenet groups, the early Internet chat rooms. Over the course of a few weeks, a motley assortment of items was posted: an autographed pair of Marky Mark underwear, a metal Superman lunchbox, computer-related hardware, and a 1952 Rolls-Royce Silver Dawn. Omidyar knew he was on to something when he sold his own broken laser pointer—clearly posted as broken—for $14 through his own site. Sotheby's it wasn't.

A fortunate series of circumstances prompted Omidyar to take AuctionWeb and transform it from a hobby into a business.

The site ran off Omidyar's personal $30-per-month account with Internet service provider Best, and as traffic increased on AuctionWeb, Omidyar started getting complaints from Best about the heavy volume to his account. The ISP contended that the programmer was actually operating a business and, despite Omidyar's protests and the fact that no money was going into his pockets, they began charging him $250 per month for a business account in 1996. Not wanting to pay that money out of his own pocket, Omidyar realized that he was going to have to charge people to use the site. He mulled it over and decided that the only people who had to pay anything were sellers, and only if they sold anything. Omidyar asked sellers to send in a payment after a sale had been completed: 5 percent on sales of less than $25, and 2.5 percent on all other transactions. That was far cheaper than the 50 percent that the average consignment store would charge, less than the 20 percent a traditional auction house charges, and could even cost less than a classified ad, depending on the newspaper and size of advertisement taken out.

The concept of charging sellers rather than buyers was more of an ad hoc solution to a problem than a real business model. In fact, Omidyar had no idea what would happen when he asked people to pay to use his little site with its dull design. If no one paid anything, he said he wouldn't have been surprised, according to Cohen's book. But pay they did. Soon he started receiving envelopes stuffed with checks or cash, including coins taped to index cards. The company had begun. Accidental or not, eBay achieved something very few online businesses managed: it actually brought in more cash than it spent from its very first days.

In AuctionWeb's first weeks, Omidyar established a philosophy built around the idea that people could be trusted, that they were basically good. If users treated others the way they themselves wanted to be treated, everything would work out fine. The philosophy worked for the most part, but when disputes arose, anyone could fire off a complaint to Omidyar. His e-mail address was right there on the site—Pierre@ebay.com—and soon he began receiving quite a bit of correspondence. Omidyar was busy with his day job and wanted to limit the time commitment of operating the auction site, so he came up with another ad hoc solution—a way to avoid dealing with the e-mails, according to Cohen. In early 1996, Omidyar gave people in the community ways to govern themselves. The Feedback Forum enabled users to leave feedback for other users as a method for earning trust. Positive performance was rewarded through a color-coded star-rating system. EBay users could also gather at the bulletin boards to share advice and resolve disputes.

Omidyar continually enhanced the features offered to users, the Feedback Forum evolved into a check-and-balance star-ratings system, and over time the items were categorized into easy-to-find sections. The online exchange began to increasingly resemble a giant swap meet, but with some distinct advantages. Unlike rummaging through a swap meet, searching on eBay for something you were looking for was easy. Additionally, using eBay's various message boards allowed you to get advice on buying or selling, much like asking a salesperson in a shop. As a seller, there was no need to go through extensive advertising to get potential customers to find you. Everything was right there in one enormous communal space open twenty-four hours a day, seven days a week.

Not only could users start searching for precisely what they wanted, but if they were unsatisfied with their interactions with someone else on the site, they could leave a negative rating along with disapproving feedback. Likewise, trustworthy buyers and sellers who delivered on their promises could reap the benefits that came with good ratings and positive feedback, building a larger following.

The eBay experience was so enjoyable that friends spread the word to each other and colleagues egged each other to start bidding. Three years after Pierre Omidyar started his Labor Day weekend project, the *St. Louis Post-Dispatch* reported that online auction fever was spreading. The excitement of bidding was catching, even addictive. Larry Horist, a longtime Lincoln enthusiast, told the *Post-Dispatch* that he became the high bidder for a Civil War–era note signed by Abraham Lincoln on eBay, offering $5,101. Horist, the paper reported, bid on the note while at work, surrounded by his coworkers.

All Horist had to do was set up a user account through eBay with his contact information. The seller who had listed the Civil War–era note had to set up a similar account, but also had to write a description of the merchandise (preferably accompanied by a photo), determine the kind of auction to launch and when to launch it, as well as what price to set. Once the seller had fielded questions from prospective buyers like Horist and the auction was over, settlement was the responsibility of both parties—Horist to pay and the seller to ship. (Later, in 2002, eBay would purchase PayPal, an online financial services company, to facilitate the transfer of payments for its auctions.)

Horist's office was hooked. "As the clock ticked off the final seconds of the auction, his office staff huddled around a computer, repeatedly clicking the RELOAD button to see if he would be outbid. When the auction closed, a small cheer went up in the room," the *Post-Dispatch* reported.

"It was like watching the final seconds of the Super Bowl. It's almost like drugs on demand, but this is auctions on demand," Horist told the paper. "I can get up in the middle of the night, turn on my computer and there are thousands of auctions going on." Other people were catching the bug, too, driven by the ease at which they could enter into the bidding. It was easy, fast, and just a click away. It became a familiar process for millions of users who have already clicked to buy something on the Internet.

In 1997, "eBay" officially became eBay.com, unveiling its new home page with the now famous red, blue, yellow, and green logo.

FROM PLUSH TO PRACTICAL

The catalyst that created the groundswell for the initial eBay craze can be attributed in part to Ty Warner, a native of the Chicago area whose parents named him after the acerbic baseball player Ty Cobb. The two Tys couldn't have been more different. Warner was an average and quiet student growing up in the Chicago suburbs. After dropping out of Kalamazoo College in Michigan, he began working for the toy company Dakin in San Francisco. He then decided to take a break from his work there and travel through Italy for a while. It's there, the story goes, that he was inspired to start his own toy company. The first toy that his company, Ty Incorporated, developed was a plush toy called the Himalayan Cat, which didn't contain very much stuffing. Although critics jeered, Warner got the last laugh. By leaving out the stuffing, the toys had an oddly appealing floppy quality. Ty's floppy cat sold more than thirty thousand units in its first run.

In 1993, Warner branched out and introduced a special line of toys made to resemble various animals. His goal was to make something small and inexpensive, something that kids could afford. The new toys contained small pellets or beans that gave them a somewhat lifelike appearance, hence their name: Beanie Babies. They were tiny, floppy, snuggly, heart-melting, and plush, and it quickly became clear that they would become irresistible. They had names like Flash the dolphin, Chocolate the moose, and Squealer the pig. Warner sought innovative channels for selling his Beanie Babies, first displaying them at the World Toy Fair in New York City and then distributing them through small shops instead of large retailers.

Reaction to the original nine Beanie Babies was positive, but it took a conscious strategy on Ty Warner's part to turn his funny little toys into a hit. The company shunned splashy ad campaigns and licensing deals, relying instead on word of mouth. Ty limited production runs and started "retiring" certain characters, causing an increased demand for the finite supply of the toys. Sales picked up as Ty added more characters to the collection. Parents and kids alike joined the hunt for elusive ones like Bronty the brontosaurus and Peanut the elephant. Eager customers lined up early in the morning outside stores, regardless of the weather conditions, just to be able to buy one.

Warner instinctively realized that the Beanie Baby popularity was fueled by a demand that was accelerated by carefully controlled supply. With each piece in such short supply, a secondary market rapidly emerged and, through a combination of luck and convenience, found a home on eBay. Both eBay and Ty Incorporated thrived off each other, and the story they were inadvertently writing together brought them more attention, pushing sales and site traffic higher and higher. By April 1997, more than 2,500 Beanie Babies were up for sale at eBay, selling for an average price of $33, even though they retailed in stores for only $5. Visitors to the site didn't want to just shop for Beanie Babies, however. They wanted to interact with other people who were as excited as they were about Buzz the bee or Brownie the bear. They used the message board to trade tips and information. The Beanie Baby community allowed eBay to grow as its users branched out into other types of trade, generating a wider selection of products and more buyers for a given item.

In May 1997, more than $500,000 changed hands through eBay in Beanie Baby transactions alone, comprising more than 6.6 percent of all eBay transactions. The dizzying volume of Beanie Baby sales at eBay unleashed a flood of media coverage that brought more people and more Beanie Babies to the site, leading to still-heavier volume. After Princess Diana died in a car crash in Paris that year, Ty asked permission from the Spencer family to release a limited edition Diana Beanie Baby. All of the proceeds from the royal purple plush bear would go to the princess's favorite charities. The catch: only stores with high-volume Beanie Baby sales would get them, and they'd get only one dozen of the bears to sell. A secondary market quickly appeared and a set of twelve bears sold for $8,300 on eBay.

One effect of the Beanie Baby craze was that a large eBay community drove business for Ty, increasing the company's revenues to the point where the reclusive Ty Warner rapidly amassed a fortune estimated at more than $5 billion by 1999. Another effect was that the phenomenon drew people who liked collecting to eBay. But a funny thing began to happen when all those people flocked to the site: they ended up exploring the site like they would a shopping mall, discovering all kinds of other products they might like to own.

The Beanie Baby phenomenon demonstrated eBay's powerful appeal to an ever growing community. Soon the crowd that had gathered at eBay in a frenzy over Beanie Babies began to now grow even faster in response to an unusual type of activity that I call the eBay "sideshow."

EBay tells its stories well, often making headlines when oddities sell on the site, sometimes for ridiculous amounts of money. The attendant publicity regularly brings in waves of new users. Special categories include "slightly unusual," "really weird," and "totally bizarre." Sometimes it seems as though there is a market for just about anything: an indie rocker's sweaty socks, a stranger's empty gum wrapper, a mounted beer-drinking armadillo. When it comes to actually plunking down good money for something absurd, eBay is the place. It reached the point where late-night comedian Jay Leno showed eBay postings to a studio audience and asked them to shout out whether they thought something had actually sold. His audience agreed that the piece of cereal that looked like ET's head should sell. They were right: it did indeed sell . . . for $786. The ET cereal, however, had nothing on the ten-year-old grilled cheese sandwich sporting scorch marks that looked like the Virgin Mary. In 2004, the stale yet sacred sandwich sold for $28,000 to an online casino.

Despite the collector stereotype it carried in its early years and the carnival antics that made it feel more like an entertainment site than a serious marketplace, eBay's site started to change as its users began experimenting with more mainstream goods. Shoppers started buying and selling computers, camera equipment, handbags, and similar ordinary items. It worked, and the nature of eBay changed forever. Today, the vast majority of eBay sales involve everyday goods. Collectibles still makes up part of the whole, but they're no longer eBay's core business. For millions of people, eBay has become as familiar and as practical as the convenience store around the corner.

NOT JUST FOR THE MAVENS ANYMORE

EBay has been compared to a large garage sale, an enormous flea market, and even a giant lemonade stand. But when you look at its scale and the scope from the enormous volume it does in everyday products, you begin to realize the absurdity of these analogies. See the chart below, which demonstrates the significance of the volume:

Ten eBay Categories Exceed $1 Billion GMS Globally

First Quarter 2004 Annualized Gross Merchandise Sales	$ Billion
Motors (eBay's automobile marketplace)	$8.7
Computers & Networking	$2.6
Consumer Electronics	$2.5
Books, Movies, Music	$2.4
Clothing & Accessories	$2.2
Sports	$2.0
Collectibles	$1.6
Home & Garden	$1.6
Toys	$1.5
Business & Industrial	$1.1

Although eBay is the established leader in consumer-to-consumer online exchanges, it wasn't the first and certainly is not the only one around. OnSale.com existed even before Omidyar's AuctionWeb. Auction Universe also emerged as an early eBay competitor, but it lacked eBay's tight-knit community and integrated message boards and failed to pull in enough users to continue. OnSale's marketing tactics backfired and it, too, lacked eBay's strong community, failing to convince enough eBay users to leave behind the reputations they had built (good ratings and positive feedback) and start anew. But then, in 1998, heavyweight Yahoo! bought out OnSale, turning it into a free exchange. The following year, online bookstore giant Amazon.com bought LiveBid.com and started its own eBay-like exchange, too. More recently, companies such as Overstock and Bidville have emerged to compete head-on. Niche players are also popping up, such as Audiogon, a specialty consumer exchange focused on the high-end audio market. Despite the presence of these companies and the certainty that new players will continue to appear, eBay is currently so pervasive and successful that it demands our attention as the representative of all online consumer secondary-market platforms. And despite the continual influx of new arrivals to the online auction scene, eBay is not only still on top of its game, but it is likely to continue being the dominant player, setting the pace for the secondary-market evolution.

Throughout its history, as the sales volume continues to grow, eBay has continued to enhance its platform. In 2000, it introduced the Buy It Now feature (BIN), offering buyers a fixed-price purchasing option akin to a traditional shopping experience. Instead of having to wait for auctions to end, the Buy It Now feature—used by itself or combined with an auction format—gave buyers the op-

portunity to purchase items from eBay at a fixed price, the way
they would buy from traditional stores. Recently, about 30 percent of all merchandise sold on eBay was sold through fixed
prices.

While eBay users have been busy "buying it now," eBay itself
has been doing the same thing. You could say that the eBay platform is even taking over the world. In 1999, eBay started acquiring online exchanges around the United States and abroad. In
addition to the classic auction platform, it now owns the online
shopping comparison service Shopping.com, the listing site
Rent.com, used-car dealer AutoTrader.com, and even a percentage of the grassroots classifieds phenom Craigslist. In 2004, eBay
went on an international shopping spree. It launched two new
sites in the Philippines and Malaysia and took over the Internet
Auction company in Korea, where half of the population of
twenty- and thirty-somethings are now registered eBay users.
The same year, eBay bought India's online auction powerhouse,
Baazee.com. (Many of the Baazee buyers and sellers prefer to set-
tle in person rather than by mail.) Soon eBay had a Dutch online
classifieds site, German online auctioneer Alando, and a percentage of the Latin American site MercadoLibre.

Now, according to its marketing figures, eBay has twenty-eight
international markets covered, including countries in the Ameri-
cas, Europe, and Asia. To give you a sense of how those markets
performed, by the third quarter 2004, 46 percent of all the goods
bought on eBay were purchased outside the United States, up
from 35 percent at the end of 2002. A twenty-something in South
Korea, a schoolteacher in France, and a computer programmer in
India could all be bidding on that Prada handbag from last year's
collection. Try reaching that range of people with a classified ad in

the local newspaper, a consignment store in your town, or even a simple advertisement on a personal Web site.

With all this growth and activity, eBay is beginning to reach orders of magnitude in volume that may surprise even avid users. An IDC analysis identified eBay as being responsible for nearly a quarter of all the e-commerce in the United States in 2004 (excluding groceries and travel). ABC News reported in 2005 that analysts estimated one out of every four dollars spent online is spent on something purchased through eBay.

The question now is where will eBay and its peers go from here. It turns out that the online auction platform still has a series of hurdles to clear.

EBAY'S FINAL FRONTIER

If you think eBay's success is impressive, view it in the context of its true potential and you will realize that it is just beginning to scratch the surface. While eBay is already clearly one of the great business ideas of all time, the company hasn't come close to reaching its full transformative potential yet. Despite eBay's ubiquitous presence, there is still a large segment of the United States and world population that has never used eBay. When the Pew Internet & American Life Project surveyed Internet users in February and March 2005, it found that the majority of the respondents had never participated in an online auction. Even more startling than the lack of overall participants is the number of eBay's users who have never sold on the site. In 2004, the *New York Times* reported that roughly 90 percent of all eBay's users are buyers, not sellers. There is a strong consensus within the business community that the number of eBay users who have never sold online is closer to 95 percent. For eBay, or any online exchange, to become transformational, there must be a better balance of buyers and sellers in the market.

So, what's holding everyone back?

One of eBay's main struggles has been its inability to ensure a consistent experience for its buyers. Take Wal-Mart as an example of a shopping fixture in our society. Each week, one third of the entire U.S. population visits a Wal-Mart store. Why? Because when a customer walks into a Wal-Mart, there is the expectation of a certain experience. Customers expect to be able to easily park nearby. Then, once they enter the store, they expect a certain variety of merchandise; a clean presentation, a particular level of service; a competitive pricing transaction at the checkout counter; where there is no worry of credit card theft; and the ability to return defective goods. Those same expectations must hold true for eBay. But today, eBay is not an easy place for transactions—the "parking lot" is far away, making it difficult and time-consuming to sell. And the experience for buyers is as inconsistent as it gets: service lacks uniformity, and dishonesty runs rampant.

By enabling his visitors to control their experiences on eBay, Omidyar gave the public control over the direction it took, for better and for worse. EBay is only as good as the people who come to do business there, and in an environment built on trust, there are inevitably going to be those who breach it. Over the past few years, eBay has been grappling with fraud and fakes, lying and cheating, which translate into an inconsistent experience for participants. Users have been known to create multiple identities and give themselves positive feedback, form alliances with other people and trade positive feedback, and band together to give someone else negative feedback—fairly or unfairly. EBay itself estimates that one out of every ten thousand listings is fraudulent, which, based on the company's own numbers, means that there are about four hundred fraudulent transactions every day on eBay. The company also noted that in 2004, PayPal lost $50.5 million to fraudulent dealings. That means that thousands of people who have had bad experiences are probably not coming back soon. And the friends and family they tell are staying away, too. Think for a moment how you would feel if you knew that a convenience store nearby was frequently getting held up by crooks. Would you go in there to shop? Probably not. That's the same kind of chilling effect dishonesty has had on eBay.

In an effort to reverse that, eBay has been addressing the challenges from dishonest people who make it unsafe to do business there. In a store, there is usually some sort of centralized control of the customer experience. Owners or managers have incentives to make sure the experiences are consistently positive, or they will lose their commissions, their customer base, their jobs, and ultimately the business itself. EBay doesn't actually sell anything. The company merely provides a platform for people to trade; therefore it can only attempt to control the experience indirectly. Today, eBay has about a thousand employees in the United States alone dedicated in some way to doing just that.

To protect consumers, eBay has an enormous Trust and Safety department responsible for ensuring a safe experience for its customers. The department employs hundreds of people authorized to monitor the community, including customer service reps and former cops. The authorities have repeatedly stepped in, nabbing eBay swindlers who do business on the site. One New Jersey man bilked buyers out of $2.5 million over the course of several years, selling them fake sports memorabilia through eBay and sports-trading magazines. The *San Diego Union-Tribune* reported that FBI agents had to ask professional baseball players whether they had signed some of the memorabilia posted on the site. They hadn't. With its active community and vibrant message boards, eBay encourages users to report similar fraud to the proper authorities, but it also discourages vigilantism, threatening to freeze the accounts of users who try to take matters into their own hands.

Another indicator that eBay has a long way to go is that the average price of items sold through the site is surprisingly low, estimated at below sixty dollars per transaction. When it becomes more secure to conduct business through eBay, not to mention easier overall, that average should rise along with an increase in liquidity.

EBay and its competitors are well aware of these barriers, and millions of dollars have been dedicated to improving the trading system. Following in the footsteps of major credit card companies, eBay has developed stronger security measures and insurance options to protect users. While there are still holes to be filled, eBay is taking steps in the right direction: offering insurance for transactions, developing new scanning software to identify illegal listings, actively policing the site, and vowing to follow up on every policy violation.

. . .

THE PHENOMENON THAT began one slow Labor Day weekend in Pierre Omidyar's apartment in California has continued to grow into a robust marketplace where a recent search for working laser pointers pulled up more than a thousand results. While eBay's success is monumental for a company that didn't exist eleven years ago, it still has a long way to go.

To facilitate realizing the full potential of the auction culture, a new genre of business has cropped up to assist us in accessing eBay and similar marketplaces. These businesses are building the bridges to allow millions of people around the world to cross into the new frontier with ease. They are the missing link to making online exchanges part of our everyday lives, and with their success we will aspire to maximize the true value of what eBay really has to offer us: a better life.

4 TRUE LIQUIDITY
Creating a Perfect Market

On a random day in 2005, eBay's stock closed at $34.50, making the company worth around $46 billion. While more than 17 million shares traded hands that day at a range of $33.81 to $34.51, there was never a difference, at any given moment, of more than a few pennies between what someone was willing to sell eBay shares for and what someone was willing to buy them for. EBay's stock is widely traded on the NASDAQ stock market, so it is considered a very liquid asset, meaning that it can be converted to cash easily at what would be widely considered a fair price. Because of this, one person's eBay stock is worth the same amount as anyone else's eBay stock anywhere in the world. Stock markets exist to ensure that stocks are liquid assets—that there is always a place you can go to buy or sell a particular stock for fair market value. EBay calls itself the World's Online Marketplace, and, along with its peers, it is aspiring to evolve into an entity that looks just like a stock market, but where people can meet to buy and sell anything at fair market value—not just stocks. Similar to the liquidity that major stock markets create for stocks, eBay and other online exchanges have the potential to create robust liquidity for thousands of types of commodities, from books to cell phones to high-end handbags to vacuum cleaners.

Today, none of the consumer-to-consumer exchanges have reached levels of activity in their marketplaces where true liquidity exists for most consumer goods. Not even eBay, with its massive user base, can be called a truly liquid marketplace yet. A quick glance at the transactions and sales of several commodities on eBay demonstrates, by contrast, the varying and inconsistent levels of liquidity that the market currently offers today. Let's look at one example. Several years ago I purchased a set of a dozen 1950s Steuben goblets from an estate sale for $1,000. Before I even got them in my car, I was approached by two glass dealers who offered me $1,800 for the set. I declined to take a quick profit because I was looking forward to enjoying the glasses, and for several years I did. But when I moved into a smaller home recently, there wasn't room for another set of stemware, so I thought it would be fun (and hopefully lucrative) to try to sell the set on eBay. The first auction I launched received ten bids and the best offer was $280, significantly less than the $1,500 reserve I had set for it, meaning that it didn't meet the amount I had designated ahead of time as the minimum price I would accept. Two weeks later, I relaunched the auction and received twenty-six bids with the highest bidder at $850. Still shy of what I thought represented fair value for the set, I put the goblets up for auction one last time and it finally found a buyer at my price.

There are several explanations for the disappointing result of my first two auctions. The right buyers may just not have been on eBay at the time, or they might have been there but were unable to find my offering because my listing didn't contain the right wording. A review of Steuben glass sold on eBay in the last year reveals that eBay is currently not a very liquid market for it. Of approximately eighteen thousand Steuben glass auctions conducted on eBay over the past twelve months, only half of them resulted in a successful transaction. Those sales generated a total of about $1.2 million.

The fact that Steuben auctions generate an average of only 4.4 bids per auction indicates that eBay has not done a good job of attracting enough buyers or sellers for Steuben's products. The data also demonstrates a mismatch between the buyers' and sellers' value perceptions. Clearly, dealers are trying to sell their wares at high prices while they are bottom-fishing for fire-sale deals from random consumer sellers like myself. At the same time, there is a limited group of affluent customers who are shopping eBay for those goods.

This phenomenon is not unique. Today, you will experience the same weak market and randomness of activity with hundreds of types of products that sellers hawk on eBay. Hermès ties don't have a formal dealer market to support a consistent price level but are considered one of, if not *the*, preeminent brands of men's neckwear. These classic ties in Fauvist colors depicting offbeat images of chess pieces, spouting whales, monkeys dodging crocodiles, and other eye-catching abstractions retail new in the store for $145 plus tax. EBay facilitates a brisk business in these snazzy ties: more than five thousand of them have sold on the site over the past year for a total of approximately $300,000. While the average tie fetched about $55, or about 38 percent of its retail price, the range was all over the place. I have watched many times as identical Hermès ties in the same condition sell for $18.50 one day and the very next week for $79.

Whenever there are consumers clamoring for a product that is hard to find, whether they are serious collectors or just casual buyers, an active community of dealers steps in to help develop a market. So it is not surprising that it's the dealer-supported commodities that are, today, most likely to achieve fair market value in the secondary markets.

In the watch market, dealers work energetically to encourage potential customers to think of watches as a valuable commodity. They advertise watches in a similar manner as the jewelry resellers do. They highlight the precious metals that watches are made from and, in the case of at least one prominent brand, reinforce the "heirloom" value. They also offer enough money on occasion to get some people digging through the attic in search of grandpa's old pocket watch. These and other efforts have continually fueled interest in watches, guaranteeing market liquidity. On any given day, at any given moment, a group of dealers will be bidding against each other for a watch on eBay, dealers who will be willing to take an inventory position even without a customer behind them, meaning they will confidently stock up on certain watches knowing that they'll be able to resell them later for a profit. Dealers go for the sure thing. They know that there will always be someone who wants to buy a watch or a crystal bowl or certain types of antiques. So, wherever there is a dealer market for a product, you can be sure that there's a built-in baseline of support for that particular product.

So how does a dealer operate? Take the case of a watch with a retail value of $1,000 that was purchased by the authorized retailer for around $600. If you wore the watch for a year and wanted to sell it back, the retailer you bought it from would probably be embarrassed to buy it back from you because he wouldn't be able to pay you anywhere near what you paid for it. After all, the store can buy the same watch new from the manufacturer for $600. Your watch is used. The store likely has plenty of inventory, so it doesn't need to invest its capital in adding another watch of the same it already has in stock. However, there are dealers who buy used watches to resell to customers that don't want to pay the premium for new watches. Those dealers compete for used watches and in doing so establish the minimum amount that the watches are worth to them. This floor price is the liquidation value of the watch—the price at which a dealer is willing to stock the item.

If the dealer has a customer lined up for the watch before he has to buy it, he will be willing to pay more for it than a dealer who has to keep it in inventory in the hope of selling it in the future. This is because one dealer has to tie up his money in the item when that money could be earning interest for him in the bank, while the other just flips the watch without laying out cash for too long.

So when you list a watch on an exchange like eBay, you should at least get the liquidation value of the item. And if you are lucky, a consumer or two will be interested in your watch and bid it up to a fairer price.

LIKE CLOCKWORK

Rolex is popularly considered one of the great pedigrees of high-end watches today. The company has a storied history—founded in 1905 by a Bavarian merchant, its watches were the first wrist pieces to be awarded official chronometer certification from the Swiss authorities—and it has benefited from a long and profitable publicity campaign, courting famous athletes and adventurers, like Everest climber Sir Edmund Hillary, as patrons. Today, roughly $6.5 million worth of Rolex watches sell on eBay every month.

In 2003, Rolex introduced a limited edition version of its popular Submariner model with a green bezel to celebrate the fiftieth anniversary of its introduction. Since it is almost impossible to buy this watch in stores today, a liquid market has formed for it on eBay. The chart below plots sales for three months of transactions on eBay for that specific watch.

Three Months' of eBay Transactions

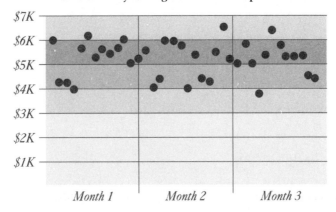

Actual transactions for all authentic Rolex Submariner fiftieth anniversary edition watches sold on eBay during a three-month period in 2005

Each dot on this chart represents an actual sale that took place over a random three-month period in 2005. The clearing price is represented on the vertical axis, and the month that it cleared in is on the horizontal access. These hard-to-get watches trade secondhand on eBay quite predictably at between $4,500 and $6,000, even though the manufacturers' suggested retail price is just under $5,000. If you are lucky to own one of these limited-edition watches and want to sell it, you can expect that you'll be able to turn it into cash within that price range relatively quickly. The market for fiftieth anniversary edition Rolex Submariners, in other words, is extremely fluid on eBay.

Aside from Rolex watches in general and some other highly prized luxury items like Louis Vuitton leather goods, Manolo Blahnik shoes, and Baccarat crystal, liquidity remains a widespread problem at eBay—so much so that eBay is often referred to as being miles wide and inches deep. There are thousands of products available in a wide variety, but most of the products don't have market depth, meaning there aren't always buyers on the site willing to offer fair market value, or sometimes any value at all. The markets for those products are therefore considered shallow and illiquid. EBay must offer broader liquidity if it is going to reach the next level of economic efficiency that will drive auction culture.

Of course, even though it's not there yet, it is quite liquid for a young marketplace. Just look back at the New York Stock Exchange, which has come a long way from the time when Wall Street was just a dirt path and traders met under a big tree to do business. The evolution of the New York Stock Exchange reads like a blueprint for how online consumer marketplaces will eventually evolve.

THE WALL STREET WAY

One of the first things Manhattan's Dutch settlers did after officially establishing New Amsterdam as a city on February 2, 1653, was to plan stronger defenses. England and Holland were at war, and the Dutch colonists had reason to be worried about a possible invasion from the British colonists in New England. So the Dutch settlers hit up their wealthiest residents to fund a palisade that was to be built with twelve-foot oak logs sunk into the ground and sharpened on the exposed end. This palisade formed a defense along part of the settlement that was wedged into the southern tip of Manhattan Island. But when the British made their move, it was by sea, and in September 1664 the Dutch surrendered New Amsterdam before a single shot was fired. The defensive wooden wall no longer served any purpose. When it was dismantled, it left behind a muddy lane that came to be known as Wall Street.

Wall Street established itself as a large center of commerce as eighteenth-century New York grew into a thriving port city, and it was there that Americans began exchanging securities informally. At this point, there were no established mechanisms for buyers and sellers to find each other, so the two groups published newspaper ads or just made a point of being seen regularly at one of the coffeehouses where trading in securities commonly took place. This informal arrangement mirrored similar ones in London and other cities around the world. They were practical but inefficient, so it was only a matter of time before the traders came up with a better system. In the spring of 1792, two dozen prominent New York stockbrokers, bankers, and merchants met under a huge buttonwood tree on Wall Street and agreed on a formal system for trading bank and insurance stocks. For lack of a better name, this would come to be called the Buttonwood Agreement, and it laid the foundation for the New York Stock Exchange. The men agreed to meet under the tree or, if the weather was especially bad, inside the Tontine Coffee House. They formed an association of Brokers for the Sale of Public Stock and kept the rules of trading simple.

The stock exchange went through its share of growing pains. The first stock traded was for the Bank of New York, which had been founded in 1784 by young American Revolution hero Alexander Hamilton. As treasury secretary, Hamilton soon found the growing trade in stocks a source of embarrassment when his assistant secretary, William Duer, became involved in an insider-trading scandal and had to quit. Duer's fall also brought down a succession of bankers and brokers, leading to panic on Wall Street. Duer and the partner he double-crossed went to debtors' prison. Hamilton, aghast at the deception, wrote, "There should be a separation between honest men and knaves, between respectable stockholders . . . and mere unprincipled gamblers," and he arranged just that.

Periodic convulsions over insider-trading excesses would plague the market throughout the years, but the story of stock trading in America expanded consistently as several waves of technological innovation led to wider and wider participation. The New York Stock Exchange was formally established in March 1817, and by 1829 trading volume had reached five thousand shares a day. The exchange received a major boost in 1844 from Samuel F. B. Morse, who transmitted the first telegraphic message, a medium that brokers quickly utilized to send and receive market quotations. By 1866 the first transatlantic cable was in place, linking brokers in New York and London. A year later, Edward Callahan invented the stock ticker, and in 1876 Alexander Graham Bell introduced the telephone, which was installed on the floor of the New York Stock Exchange for the first time in November 1878. These and other innovations helped push daily volume ever higher; it exceeded a million shares for the first time on December 15, 1886.

The advent of greater and easier participation in the stock exchange brought dramatic improvements in market liquidity because the only way to create a highly liquid market is to have large numbers of actively involved buyers and sellers. The measure of a market's liquidity usually comes down to a calculation of how often a product is bought and sold, or in the case of the stock market, the number and size of trades, which is always closely monitored. The greater the volume, the deeper the liquidity, and therefore the less the risk of paying a disadvantageous price.

FACILITATING LIQUIDITY

The lesson of the stock market is that true market liquidity only comes with years of refinement and active participation from a variety of facilitators. Thousands of brokers, traders, expediters, analysts, bankers, and floor runners have made the stock market what it is today. Imagine what our investment portfolios would be worth today had it not been for the assistance of companies like Merrill Lynch or Charles Schwab that helped us access the markets easily and at a relatively low cost. Were it not for the facilitators behind every trade, we'd still be stuck in the early Wall Street days; one person's stock in IBM might be worth $100 at the same time that another's is worth $20.

On the heels of the Depression, financier Charles Edward Merrill revolutionized the modern stock market by working to combat the exclusivity of Wall Street. He opened hundreds of brokerage branches across the country and empowered the new middle class with the investment tools they'd need to make informed decisions. He organized investment seminars with accompanying child care for parents who wanted to learn about the stock market, and he even coined the phrase "bringing Wall Street to Main Street" to describe his philosophy. Merrill connected his branch offices in different cities to the main office by Teletype, an electric apparatus similar to the typewriter that functioned as a kind of rudimentary message system similar to the way we use e-mail today. The subsequent news that flowed through the wires made for informed brokers and instilled customers with a sense of confidence in the firm.

Before there were stockbrokers, shareholders actually had to physically go somewhere to find a buyer if they wanted to sell their stock, an arduous process that bore a high transaction cost. Today, armies of middlemen provide a link between buyers and sellers to facilitate activity. And the supplemental contributions of research analysts, economists, estate planners, and other financial service providers to the knowledge pool give average Joes access to the kind of information they need to make wise investment decisions. Accessing the financial markets is getting easier every day. A few years ago, we traded stocks by phone. Now most companies let you execute trades automatically with just a click on their Web site.

Looking back, the volume of stocks traded in the 1920s seems puny compared to where the market is now. Compared to the nearly 224 million shares traded on the New York Stock Exchange in all of 1926, for example, the daily—*daily*—volume averaged more than a billion shares in 2004. It's a level of activity based on a level of liquidity that would have been truly unimaginable to the founders of the exchange.

MISSED OPPORTUNITIES

Though secondary-market liquidity for consumer goods still has a long way to go before it begins to approximate the stock market's, there is undoubtedly money to be made in it. Remember the ACNielsen survey that revealed that an average of $2,200 of stuff you once purchased is just gathering dust in your home? Analysts have concluded that the total "eBay value" of these dusty belongings exceeds $1,000—not a perfect translation of worth, but still quite a bit of money, considering that, after taxes, the average American household usually puts approximately $5,000 a year into discretionary spending on things like alcohol, eating out, and entertainment, according to the Bureau of Labor Statistics. If each family can add $1,000 to their base of discretionary income, they will increase their spending base by 20 percent annually. With more than $1,000 buried in roughly 120 million American households, that's more than $120 billion dollars just waiting to be mined. And that's just the average. As you move up the socioeconomic ladder, the numbers grow exponentially in concert with wealth and spending.

One would think that kind of windfall would draw nearly everybody into the online auction arena, but the investment—meaning the time it takes to learn how to sell and to process sales on these exchanges—has so far discouraged the masses from actually going through the motions.

Selling on eBay is just way too difficult.

Remember my Steuben glassware? The prospect of fluctuating bids is maddening enough, but in order to even get to that point, there are too many hoops to jump through. The selling process has been eBay's Achilles' heel.

A new seller has to start by gaining access to the Internet. We might think that these days every American logs on to the Internet regularly, but there's still a percentage of the population that doesn't have easy access. The most recent U.S. Census Bureau reports show that nearly 40 percent of American households still don't have computers and Internet access.

But access is only one prerequisite. Once you've logged on, you'll need to spend time registering on eBay. You'll need to figure out a handle and a password, and you'll need to possess a valid credit card—not to be charged, just to sign up. Without one, you're pretty much out of luck because most sellers use a financial system that requires credit to trade. Then you'll have to familiarize yourself with eBay's setup, learning the ins and outs of your account and the way the entire site works. However simple that might sound, it takes time. Basically, you'll have invested several hours just to move up the learning curve enough to use the site.

Online auctions are like online personals: it's a rare shopper who will spring for something he or she can't see. That means you will need to get a digital camera to take photos of what you are selling to upload to your listing. If you don't own a digital camera already, prepare to invest even more time. Not familiar with megapixels? How about which brand to buy? You've got your research cut out for you. Keep in mind that blurry and pixelated photos raise suspicions in a market awash with fake versions of everything. Then, don't forget to photograph the inside of your designer bag, its label, detailing, and other aspects of your belongings to demonstrate authenticity—all from different angles. Photos that don't convey any sense of scale or that misrepresent your item will reap buyer ire.

Assuming you have an Internet-enabled computer and a digital camera, you now have to actually process the auction. Which category, precisely, does your item fall into? Do you want to pay to list it in multiple categories? How about springing for a border around your listing to draw attention to it? What about paying extra so that potential buyers can view a larger, more detailed version of your photos? New sellers are limited to the basic bid-style auction, whereas advanced sellers can set up a fixed-price option with the proprietary Buy It Now feature. What's your reserve price? Do you even want a reserve? How long do you want your listing posted (seven days assures you the weekend shoppers)? What's the opening bid going to be (the lower that price, the more bidders you might attract)? Before you click SUBMIT, consider the time of day and day of week of when you will be launching your auction as well as when it will end (did you know that Sundays are great for ending auctions for women's clothing; evenings are good for watches; any time and day for collectibles, except Friday night and Saturday, when people are traditionally away from their computers; and regardless of time or day, holidays are always best avoided). You should also have brushed up on your writing skills as you will want to be detailed in your description of the product. Good photos and copy can mean the difference between attracting a few dozen prospective buyers or only a few.

Then, if your images and item description aren't completely self-explanatory (and no matter how clear you think you've been, they never are), you'll be fielding questions from prospective buyers for the duration of the auction process. What is the actual length of the waist of the jeans being sold? Is that a scratch on the silver or just a buff mark? Could you send me a detailed shot of the back of the watch so I can verify the serial number? Can you tell me the reserve? The questions go on and on. And if you're not instantly responsive, the buyers are on to the next auction.

Once the auction closes you must make payment arrangements. You could just ask for buyers to send money orders, cashier checks, or other types of payments that don't require a credit card, but if the item is expensive you might find yourself setting up a secure transaction through a facilitator like Escrow.com, a leading company that provides such a service. That's another password-protected account you need to walk through and set up. You also need to learn how to set up your account to accept credit card payments or open a PayPal account. When, after you manage to sell something to someone, anyone, and you've chased down the payment, you'll have to ante up between 5 and 8 percent in seller fees to eBay for having served as the platform for the transaction.

Then you have to find a box to package your item, schlep down to the local post office or Mail Boxes Etc., and ship it directly to the buyer quickly to secure positive feedback.

Yes, selling on eBay or any of the other online exchanges is not easy—not at all.

And it gets worse.

If you have never sold on eBay before, you won't have any customer-satisfaction feedback, so your status as a law-abiding citizen on the exchange will be questionable. Without any feedback, it will be difficult to find a buyer who will trust you and pay anything close to maximum value for whatever you are selling. Building trust is an essential part of eBay. Buyer feedback is as valuable as money itself. It can take many transactions and a lot of time to establish yourself and build feedback.

Given these considerations (or, perhaps more accurately, limitations), it makes no sense at all for most people to sell directly on eBay!

In economic terms, the transaction cost to sell on eBay is quite high as measured by the opportunity cost. Opportunity cost—the time that is required to make a sale, multiplied by the value of your time—can turn out to be greater than the expected value received once the good is sold. Was it really worth going through that painstaking process to get $15 for an old purse or a picture frame? If it takes you three hours to run an auction from start to finish and you earn $20 an hour in your regular job, you want to be grossing at least $60 from your sale to just break even. Now throw in all the technical investments (camera, etc.) and the packaging and shipping fees. If the Nike sneakers you are selling are expected to fetch only $30, you are theoretically losing money before you even start. The startling fact is that if you earn more than around $32,000 annually at your job, the only reason you should be selling directly on eBay is if the item you are selling is very expensive or you enjoy the process enough to do it as a hobby.

It's no wonder eBay hasn't reached the next level of its potential—it hasn't been able to convince more than a small percentage of its users to actually sell something on its site. But things are about to change in a dramatic way. A new generation of online auction facilitators have cropped up and are transforming the marketplace. Some of these eBay facilitators may be new Merrill Lynches and Charles Schwabs and all of them will soon change the way we buy and sell goods forever.

SHOP, DROP, AND SHOP SOME MORE

Right now, plenty of buyers use eBay largely for fun. Some troll the site every day, some rummage on weekends, and some drop in randomly when they have a free moment. EBay is probably not at the forefront of your thoughts when you think of shopping for new shoes (or used ones, for that matter). In fact, you might never have thought of buying used shoes—"slightly used"—at all. When online auction facilitators become mainstream, they will enable eBay to become not just a popular destination for entertainment but a regular part of our lives as well.

Facilitators are a natural extension of the first users who took to eBay with wild enthusiasm, sharing advice and experience despite the site's drawbacks. For nearly as long as eBay has existed, a small community of knowledgeable and enthusiastic sellers has offered to sell items for their friends and family members. This casual arrangement evolved into a practice wholly supported by eBay. In 2002, eBay rolled out the Trading Assistant program, which promotes experienced members who, for a fee, help newcomers process their auctions. More than fifty thousand professional assistants have taken on the role of eBay trade facilitators worldwide. Similarly, other entrepreneurs have developed business services to assist would-be buyers who would otherwise have never attempted to unload their belongings through an online auction in a variety of ways.

Early in the gold-rush days of the dot-com boom, a handful of forward thinkers recognized the need for facilitation and attempted to become the middlemen for prospective eBay sellers. They started businesses that provided a service where customers could bring their items to a storefront and have other people take care of selling them on eBay in exchange for a percentage of the final sale. Phillip Davies tried to take TIAS.com, his Web site dedicated to antiques and collectibles trading, to the public through mobile carts at malls across America intended to help dealers post their merchandise on the Internet. But it took too long to achieve sales, and by then the revenues weren't worth it. "The hard part was nailing down all the data on all this stuff, taking it from the brick-and-mortar world and dumping it into eBay," Davies told the *New York Times* in 2003. TIAS still exists, but not as a dropshop. Another innovator, MyEZSale.com, was a venture-backed business that arrived on the scene in 2000 with a partnership that included a number of small Internet company franchises across the United States. The company equipped about two hundred pack-and-ship stores across Denver and New England with dropshop capabilities, relying on the customers to come to them. Two years later, however, MyEZSale collapsed, closing down its in-store kiosks after burning through millions of venture capital dollars. As with any consignment-like business, a drop-off store can only do as well as the value of the items that come through its door.

Most likely these pioneers just started out too early, before both the technology and user community were there to support them, like da Vinci sketching a helicopter. Starting around 2003, however, the market became ripe for an entrepreneur to try the concept again. Russ Grove is one of several of the more publicized second-generation brokers in the eBay dropshop world. A computer aficionado, Grove was an early eBay adopter, but as soon as he tried to sell items on the site, he experienced the amount of energy it involved, so he came up with a franchise model for a drop-off store called NuMarkets, which was supported by software he developed that made the processing of eBay auctions inexpensive and scalable. "Every business has its place. You and I can cook the cheeseburger at home and every restaurant in town cooks them, and then there's McDonald's," Grove says. "We're trying to become the McDonald's of this industry, if you will."

The growing pains NuMarkets experienced—like those inflicted by archaic laws in Tennessee predating the Internet that nearly required the company's participation in a live cattle auction before its auction license could be processed—are a good indication of just how novel the concept was. But now it's not difficult to see the drop-off stores expanding everywhere in the future, in support of a global marketplace. NuMarkets recently sold a special kind of early American wooden table found in Tennessee to a buyer in Portugal for $1,000. When Grove pointed out to the seller that it would cost $1,400 to ship, the buyer said, "Young man, you try to find early Americana over here in Portugal!" Now, because of a streamlined back-end system, NuMarkets claims that it is able to process items in three to seven minutes on average. The fact that it will accept almost anything from Incredible Hulk figurines to full wooden organs to Depression-era ashtrays has earned NuMarkets consideration by many as "the garage sale" of dropshops.

Another early dropshop company, AuctionDrop, took a similar approach to the business when it was started by Internet

Shopping Network founder Randy Adams along with two Silicon Valley business veterans in 2003. The company sales offering has become the standard model for this type of service.

The store accepts items of a certain minimum worth—in AuctionDrop's purview, that's at least $75—and that are under 25 pounds. The staff takes professional digital photographs of the item, lists a seven-day auction on eBay, responds to questions about the item, and eventually ships it to the winning bidder. In exchange for their services, the dropshop gets between a 20 and 40 percent cut when an item sells, depending on the final value of the item. The balance is sent to the original owner. Whenever something doesn't sell, the company can relist it, ship it back to the owner, or arrange to have it donated to charity.

AuctionDrop expanded from a San Francisco Bay–area business to a national one, quickly spreading to thousands of other locations across the country when the company signed a deal with UPS in 2004. The partnership has created more than 3,800 locations nationally where you can now drop off your things for sale online. The company is effectively pulling in entirely new sellers to the secondary market; more than 80 percent of AuctionDrop's customers have never sold anything on eBay before and about 18 percent don't even have a computer.

AuctionDrop competitor QuikDrop also started up in 2003 with the simple creed, "We sell your stuff on eBay!" The Quik-Drop franchise, currently based in Carson City, Nevada, evolved out of a Web site hosting service called Quik Internet. QuikDrop positions its storefronts near grocery stores and pharmacies to maximize convenience and ships the items it gathers directly from its storefronts instead of from a central location. Another recent entrant onto the scene is iSold It, a dropshop franchise that has opened at least one hundred stores nationwide since its 2003 inception and has plans to open several hundred more in a year's time. The company claims to be the highest-volume eBay drop-off store in America today.

Dropshops have now sprung up all over the United States and even abroad. According to ECommerce-Guide.com, "Auction drop-off stores now number 7,000 across the United States, with no end to their explosive growth in sight." The largest and most visible are independent and franchise players, with locations ranging from under a hundred to thousands, including AuctionDrop, iSold It, QuikDrop, Snappy Auctions, and NuMarkets—all aimed at the eBay auction venue. EBay itself even lists these stores, in part to promote use of the site, and in part to steer sellers to reputable companies for help. And dropshops aren't just for the uninitiated. Even for people who know how to sell on eBay, drop-off stores save them precious time.

Although dropshops serve to eliminate the hassles of selling online, they haven't fully addressed the issue of how to deal with luxury goods and valuable collectibles. More expensive items require specialized expertise to appraise, authenticate, and auction. Imagine reviewing an auction on eBay for a diamond tennis bracelet that has a $2,000 starting price. It's something that you really want and the price will certainly be lower than buying it at a jewelry store. You are about to make a bid, when suddenly you are filled with trepidation. What if this item isn't what they say it is? What if the diamonds are fake? What does the seller even know about the item? The higher the asking price, the louder these questions get, and the more you'll need to be comfortable with the seller to buy it. However, if the item is listed by a drop-shop with an extremely positive feedback rating that also has the necessary expertise to authenticate it, there's a good chance you'll buy it.

Most dropshops don't have specific levels of expertise for the items they handle. They're generalists and, as a buyer, you are relying on their integrity to ship an item after you buy it as well as their common sense to identify the obvious—like testing a digital camera they receive to make sure it works before selling it. One company that has successfully merged the processing service levels of a dropshop with the expertise of an auction house is my company, Portero. In fact, it was Portero's forward-looking business model that initially drew me to it.

My business partner, Portero co-founder Michael Sheldon, a former venture capitalist, had bought and sold on eBay ever since the online auction's early days, when, he says, it was a much more innocent and community-oriented place. Then a dramatic increase in eBay users was accompanied by a corresponding increase in fraud and seller misrepresentation. Sheldon saw how counterfeit products in the image of top luxury brands like Hermès and Tiffany were being pawned on eBay, affecting the prestigious brands' reputations. The rampant fraud had a negative effect on innocent buyers, too, who opened their packages only to find that they'd essentially been robbed. Sheldon saw an opportunity to establish a trusted national brand in the luxury goods and collectibles markets. He had watched how Mercedes-Benz took control of its luxury brand in the 1980s, moving its used vehicles from used-car lots back to its dealer lots under the label Certified Pre-Owned. He thought that other companies could do this in the online auction arena by partnering with a dropshop that guaranteed authenticity. Sheldon started out by opening a test store in upscale Greenwich, Connecticut, but he quickly realized that the traditional drop-off store model needed some fine-tuning.

A successful investment professional had received a Portero brochure in the mail and decided to give the dropshop a try. On a warm Saturday morning, he went down to his basement and hauled up eight items, including a cardboard box packed with twenty vintage license plates, a large computer monitor from the mid-nineties, an antique rocking chair, some old appliances, and two cast-iron flower planters. He loaded them into his car, drove to the Greenwich dropshop, and brought the eight items in with him. Portero doesn't accept items worth less than about $200 because each auction requires so much intensive work to prepare. Portero employees researched the value of each of the eight items, and after about forty minutes the man learned that they could sell only four of the pieces.

"This poor guy had to put half the items back in his car and take them back to his basement," Sheldon said. "The four that we took sold well, but that is not the point. The point is that, for a busy professional, this was not a good experience." Sellers like him don't want to be bothered to sort through their attics and carry everything to a storefront, Sheldon thought, so he changed Portero's model. The company, which is now headquartered in Armonk, New York, makes house calls and picks up items directly from clients' homes in major cities. It services affluent communities throughout the country through a direct sales force and affiliates and focuses exclusively on luxury goods and collectibles. Its employees, numbering about fifty, gather items for auction that are generally worth $400 on average, many times the average price of an item sold on eBay. Portero bills itself as "eBay for the affluent" and is widely recognized as the premier luxury player on the platform.

While the diverse dropshop phenomenon continues to spread across America, drop-off stores have also been cropping up overseas. Germany has DropShop, London has Auctioning4u and AuctionAssist, and several American franchises have moved into the dropshop void abroad as well. "Culturally, people are a lot more conservative," Sien Trang of AuctionAssist told the London *Guardian* in 2004. "It has the potential to be quite explosive once people accept that it is something that you do." International dropshops are the start of an entirely new business genre: the online auction facilitator.

To a certain extent, the dropshop phenomenon is viral like eBay was, in that it's not driven by big advertising but rather by local word of mouth. Clearly they are the harbingers of a whole new ecosystem of businesses whose sole purpose is to make selling in the secondary market easier. These facilitators, which already come in many shapes and sizes, will become staple consumer services in every community. When I first started putting my ideas together for this book, few people had even heard about drop-off stores. As I got down to the writing, I caught an increasing number of mentions in the media about this interesting new idea. Then, in January 2005, the message came through loud and clear. You know you've reached the mainstream when *Cosmopolitan* magazine publishes an article on "24 Ways to Simplify Your Life" with the recommendation to "Cash In Your Crap." "Does the thought of spending an entire Saturday having a yard sale sound less than appealing?" the magazine asked. "Well, you're in luck. There are thousands of eBay drop-off stores popping up all over the country. Places like QuikDrop, Cyber Listers, and City-girl Boutique will auction off your goods (for a small profit) and send you a check when they make the sale." Now there are thousands of these stores opening up all over the world.

This wide range of facilitators will dramatically increase market liquidity on eBay by making selling online cost effective as well as socially acceptable. With one of these stores in every community in the country—and eventually the world—we will naturally migrate to them and they'll become an errand that we naturally run, the same way we stop by the dry cleaners or the bank now. As simple as the concept of these stores is, it's revolutionary—just as revolutionary as the brokers that emerged to make the stock market accessible to the average investor. And like the researchers, economists, and estate planners who provide the average investor with the information he or she needs to make fruitful investments, there will be similar facilitators to advise average consumers when and how to access the secondary markets. Imagine knowing exactly what price your old dishes will fetch online or how much you can expect to get by unloading that old camera in your attic. Look around your home and take a closer look at the clothes you bought recently, the new gadget you impulsively purchased, and the most expensive things you own. Now picture trading them in for something even better a few months down the line at minimal cost to you. Welcome to the new auction culture.

5 FUTURE VALUE
Embracing the Auction Culture

With thousands of facilitators putting up shingles on every town's Main Street and drop-off-stores as ubiquitous as Starbucks, the hassle of selling our goods will disappear. It will become just as easy to sell things as it now is to buy them. All we'll have to do is *want* to take advantage of the opportunity. Some people will jump in quickly, lining up right away with used but useful items. Others will hold back, waiting to see how it all goes before taking the plunge. A few will take advantage of the opportunity to off-load their own things, but will remain wary of buying other people's slightly used goods. And then there will be bargain shoppers who will spot deals on coveted brands, readily pouncing on "temporarily owned" finds.

As the secondary market grows, a key set of changes will encourage more participation. The first major change will be one of awareness. As dropshops become more visible and more sellers start telling their neighbors, colleagues, and friends about the great deals they've made by unloading their relics, more of us will be convinced to take a fresh look at our own possessions. The dropshop veterans will teach us not only about the value we stand to gain outright from selling, but also of the value we stand to gain by "trading up" to buy what we really wanted but was previously out of reach. "Dropshopping" will be more than the matter of convenience it is today. It will be a practice that not only gets the new blouse or iPod shipped to your door overnight, but that gives you the means to buy nicer things more frequently because you'll be thinking about value in a new way.

When we're successful at attaining things that we otherwise would never be able to afford or even find, we have the tendency to broadcast the news. As more of us hear about great deals from friends who have been happy with their experiences, more of us will swarm sites like eBay.

A WEDDING STORY (WITH MANOLOS)

A friend of mine recently went through the emotional (and expensive) process of marrying off his oldest daughter. He would call me every week or so and give me updates on all the details he had to worry about—and they were considerable. If you haven't gone through the process of planning an elaborate wedding, you can't imagine how much attention and worry goes into getting every last detail just right.

This friend has done very well for himself, and he intended to spare no expense for his daughter. He rented the beautiful grand ballroom at the Plaza, the former landmark hotel for weddings in

New York City, and ordered only the finest champagne and the finest food. He bought up half the flowers in New York City. His daughter went from designer to designer and finally found the perfect wedding gown, which set him back a good deal more than he'd expected. He never complained about the money or even thought about saying no, until his daughter came to him to talk about shoes.

She had decided that the only way to do justice to her beautiful wedding dress was to wear one very specific pair of ivory Manolo Blahnik shoes beaded with iridescent flowers that sell for more than $800.

"For shoes!" my friend kept repeating. "That's insane."

I thought about trying to explain to him that Manolo Blahniks are special shoes, that they have been the footwear of choice for young women of distinction for the past thirty years: Charlotte Rampling, Marisa Berenson, and Jane Birkin—not to mention the obsession of uber–material girl and pop culture princess Carrie Bradshaw, the main character on the television series *Sex and the City*. I might have considered mentioning that Blahnik himself—a one-time set designer turned ladies footwear manufacturer at the behest of Diana Vreeland—is widely considered the world's greatest shoe designer.

But none of this background would likely have helped him understand his daughter's insistence on Manolos. No matter who bought them or made them or loved them, or wore them on television, he had an unexplainable psychological problem with the price. His monthly car lease payment was greater than most people's rent and he spent more on a suit than people often do on a family vacation. But spending $800 for a pair of shoes that his daughter would wear only once seemed insane.

So he was pretty happy to learn that he didn't really have to.

I asked him: what if you knew that she could wear the shoes down the aisle and then sell them the following week for $600? In essence, he would be leasing the shoes—the perfect shoes for the occasion, the ones that would really please his daughter, and really paying only $200. That's quite a bargain for perfection.

Manolos for a bargain? Even my friend could see the sanity in that.

I explained the opportunities that companies like eBay and their facilitating businesses are creating and how it's now possible to do something like sell a pair of "once worn" shoes to someone who's happy to get a $200 discount and will love them almost as much "like new" as she would have if she took them home in a shiny white box from Madison Avenue. Not only did his daughter get her perfect wedding shoes, but he called me back a few days later to ask what I thought he could get for a collection of gold-plated Dunhill lighters gathering dust in a drawer since he had stopped smoking two years earlier. I can't remember what I predicted, but they fetched more than $1,000 on eBay.

FOUND VALUE

My friend's house, as with so many homes, turned out to be pretty full of unused stuff worth reselling. As soon as he understood that a resale market existed, he started to search through the "junk spaces"—the attic, the basement, closets—looking for value.

That's how most of us will begin embracing this new lifestyle—we'll unearth scraps of value that are lying around and gathering dust in our lives, like my skis. The ACNielsen study tells us that a typical U.S. household has sixteen unused items lying around. Consider what unknown gems might be hidden in your home:

Found Value of Products

Found Value Hidden in Your Closet, Garage, Attic	August 2005 Price on eBay:
Gucci handbag from five years ago	$450.00
Manolo Blahnik shoes that pinch	$205.00
Last year's St. John suit	$305.00
Hermès scarf bought in Paris three years ago	$187.00
Nokia cell phone from recent upgrade	$87.00
Used Sony digital camera	$197.00
Three-year-old IBM Thinkpad notebook	$223.00
Unwanted Swarovski crystal figurine wedding gift	$128.00
Gibson guitar that hasn't been played since college	$700.00
Inherited Rosenthal china from Grandma	$575.00
Old Tumi luggage that has just been replaced	$210.00
Women's Riedell ice skates bought on a whim	$137.00
Tiffany silver heart bracelet from an ex	$58.00
Wacky Packages sticker collection from childhood	$120.00
Old Miele vacuum cleaner from last apartment	$200.00
$150 store credit at Macy's for returned gifts	$130.00
Rossignol cross-country skis	$40.00
Panasonic boom box that predates current stereo	$50.00
Old set of Ping i3 golf clubs	$347.00
Treadmill used as clothes hanger for two years	$227.00
Maui Jim sunglasses	$92.00
Collection of five XBox video games	$50.00
Electric drill	$25.00
Total found value on eBay	**$4,773.00**

Sources: eBay, Portero

That list of items may be enticing enough, but consider also that as the secondary market grows, prices will become more and more competitive; we'll be able to get closer and closer to the true residual value in selling our goods.

As we've seen, the supply of merchandise has generally been sporadic, unpredictable, and largely uncontrollable in the secondary market channels up to now (even on eBay), and that has kept the average prices for most items artificially low—the result of a limited number of shoppers being attracted to such venues as a regular place to shop. The potluck nature of flea market and garage sale inventory always prevented those venues from competing with department stores for your day-to-day shopping needs, and the same force has been at work in limiting the use of eBay. But as eBay and its competitors grow and provide a broader and more steady stream of inventory, they will attract larger and more diverse groups of potential buyers. As a result, we can expect to see prices generally increase in parallel in the short run.

We might expect that a higher supply of goods will lead to lower prices, according to basic supply and demand theory, and that will ultimately be true for the secondary online marketplace. But in this initial growth phase, prices in general will be driven up because more and more buyers will enter the market and bid for items faster than new sellers can list their goods. A larger, and therefore more competitive, buying community makes sellers more likely to earn fair market value for their goods, thereby enticing them to enter the market.

If a seller has thirty serious buyers interested in her item, she's likely to get a higher price for it than she would with only three, so average prices are bound to increase in the short run as the marketplace grows into a mainstream destination to shop.

The big (and novel) opportunity inherent in a consumer-to-consumer marketplace like eBay is that all of the buyers possess the potential to become sellers. As we, the buyers, watch the prices going up, there will come a point when we're bound to consider crossing over to the other side and joining the marketplace as sellers, since the more cash we can get for something we own, the more likely we are to sell it.

More sellers will enter the market as they fall out of love with their most recent acquisitions, realizing how much their slightly used possessions are worth and contemplating the new purchases they can make with the newfound money. And the increasing supply will attract more and more buyers. It's a virtuous cycle that will push prices higher and higher (encouraging more people to embrace auction culture and sell) until products either reach their fair secondary market value or supply begins to outpace demand.

TO HAVE, BUT NOT TO HOLD

The more developed the secondary marketplace becomes, the more profound its effects on our consumer behavior will become. It will begin to affect not only the way we think about the things we already own but don't use, but will also shape the way we think about the things we actually do use and shape our expectations about what we will allow ourselves to buy.

Our possessions, perhaps even our newest and favorite acquisitions, will become assets we can trade. The key difference will be that we'll think in terms of temporary ownership, realizing that we ought to keep many of our things for a relatively short time and be sure to sell them while there's still a good resale market for them. One of the profound truths of the resale market, even today, is that the highest volume of sales, by far, is of goods that are in the "in-season retail" category, meaning goods that are so new that they're still considered current. The following chart shows how striking the concentration of sales in this category is:

Current Secondary Market Activity Over a Product's Life Cycle

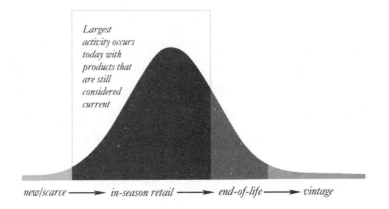

Largest activity occurs today with products that are still considered current

new/scarce ⟶ *in-season retail* ⟶ *end-of-life* ⟶ *vintage*

Right now we tend to think of the value of our possessions as either the price we pay when we buy them new or their worth when we no longer want them, which is zero dollars. But an item's value is actually changing all the time, and in the secondary-goods market, the value generally decreases precipitously over time, unless of course the item is a collectable. Knowing how to gauge when is the right time to sell our goods in order to get both the optimal amount of use out of them and the best resale value for them will be the trick. And that will all depend upon our understanding of the utility of our goods to us by comparison to the changing market value we could get for them. Take a case in point.

I recently bought a new BlackBerry personal digital assistant (PDA), and can anticipate that its value over time will look something like this:

PDA Value over Time

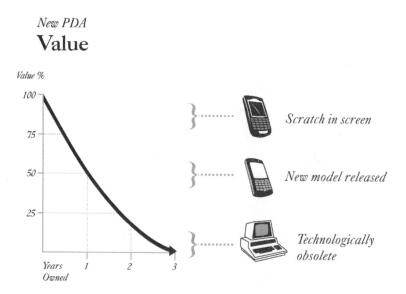

New PDA
Value

Value %

100

75

50

25

Years Owned   1   2   3

Scratch in screen

New model released

Technologically obsolete

Every time I drop the device or scratch the screen, its value will decrease. In the meantime, the value will also be decreasing because BlackBerry and its competitors—Sidekick, Palm, and others—will develop newer technology and introduce novel features in future models. (I was recently told by a reliable source that our cell phones will soon project images on our walls and ceilings!) Similarly, when the inevitable scuff marks begin to crowd the toes of your pair of Manolos and when Manolo puts out his next collection of shoes featuring a more current color scheme and a more modern heel design, the value of your shoes decreases.

At the same time as the value is changing, an object's utility—the benefit, or satisfaction, we get from owning our shoes or using our BlackBerries—also decreases. The utility of our belongings is based on many ways in which they are of use to us, factors such as the way a pair of shoes make us look and feel, or how efficiently a PDA lets me conduct business from outside my office. We typically derive less satisfaction and less utility from most possessions over time. Remember that expensive digital camera I purchased? I was snap-happy in the beginning, but eventually I stopped using the camera altogether. The decrease in utility may be less extreme for many of the goods we buy, but almost all of them lose a good deal of their utility after only a couple of years. For example, as fashions change, we are much less likely to wear the clothes we bought even just a year or two ago. Per the chart below:

Declining Utility over Time

Designer Shoes
Utility

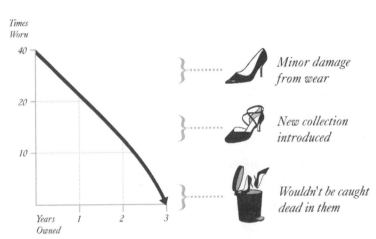

Times Worn

40

20

10

Years Owned   1   2   3

Minor damage from wear

New collection introduced

Wouldn't be caught dead in them

As savvy consumers, we're accustomed to comparing something's value and its utility right at the moment of purchase, when we decide that the utility of a purchase is greater or equal to the item's cash value. When I try on a beautiful cashmere sweater and look at myself in the dressing room mirror, do I feel like a million dollars? What I'm really asking myself subtly is if I feel good enough in it to spend the $400 it costs. This is the same process that we'll start to employ naturally in order to determine what and when to sell. If a pair of shoes stops making me feel good when I wear them, I stop wearing them. They have zero utility to me, but they may still have market value because they could have utility for someone else. If that's the case, then in the new economy of the auction culture, I should sell the shoes. In the past, we probably didn't lose much value by keeping those shoes, because the secondary markets were so inefficient. Selling the shoes at a garage sale or through a consignment shop back then wouldn't have brought in much of a return.

The value and utility of our belongings still decrease independently, but now the two lines intersect because the retrievable value for them has risen. Say you decide to buy a clean-cut suit at your local department store. It costs you a few hundred bucks and its understated dark gray makes you feel good when you wear it. In the beginning, you wear the suit almost weekly. The following year it's still in fashion, but you choose it less frequently when you look in your closet in the morning—there are now others that you prefer. A few years after that, you've gained twenty pounds, the entire style of suits has changed, and the color doesn't even go with the latest shirts and ties on sale. Your suit might still be in good shape, but its usefulness to you has changed.

In the old consumer culture, unless your suit was of such fine
quality that a consignment shop would take it in, the chance that
you could find somebody who wanted it, was the same size as you,
and was willing to give you meaningful value to take it off your
hands was, well, quite slim. Without a liquid market, the practical
value of the suit went to zero pretty quickly. Chances are the suit
wound up getting handed down to a just-out-of-college nephew
or being donated to a charitable agency like Goodwill.

Here's a graph that depicts how, before the secondary markets started to become more liquid, the utility of an item and its
value both declined over time. As discussed, the value declined
much more rapidly than its utility.

Value vs. Utility: Pre-Auction Culture

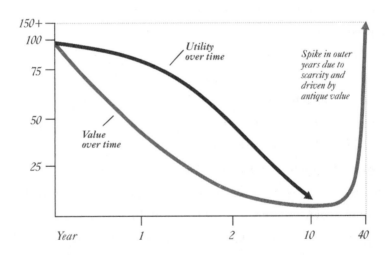

But with the development of the secondary market, that
graph looks like this:

Value vs. Utility: Post-Auction Culture

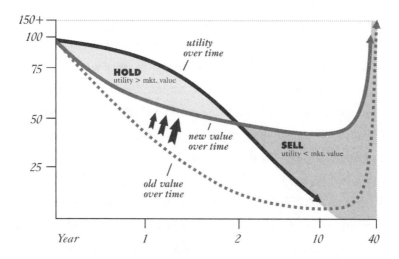

The suit's value still depreciates, but the existence of liquidity in the secondary market means that it declines more slowly and that it ultimately declines less. The optimal time to sell our goods will be when the two lines meet—when an item's utility to us declines to the point where it dips below the price someone else will pay us for the item in the secondary market. Once we internalize this way of thinking about the goods we buy, our consumer behavior will be profoundly affected. It's the same as figuring out a gratuity or estimating the sale price of a jacket—sometimes we trace numbers in the air to figure them out, but the inclination to come up with an answer has become second nature to us.

I am a gadget junkie. I'm an experimenter—I love to try new things, and I know that, frequently, I'm more entertained by the novelty of an object and by the process of experimenting than I am by whatever its functionality might be. I know that when I take home a new "toy," a good part of the value I'm getting is in the satisfaction of my impulse to try something new. Once I have satisfied my curiosity, I get bored and the value, or utility, of what I just purchased diminishes. In the last year this appetite has been piqued with a hodgepodge of items that included a scooter from the Sharper Image that I spotted in a store window, a gas-powered off-road radio-controlled car that I read about in a magazine and ordered off a Web site, and a soldering iron I saw on a TV infomercial that instantly heats up to melt solder and then instantly cools down to the point where it can be touched within seconds. I had to have all of them. The scooter was fun for a few rides. The soldering iron is still cool, but I don't really have anything to solder. I used the radio-controlled car all last summer and had a blast feeling like a kid again with it. But now they are all gathering dust when they could be enjoyed by someone who will appreciate them. I still own all three, in large part because I feel guilty that I didn't get enough use out of them. In the future, the only guilt I will feel is the guilt associated with having allowed the items to lose value when I could have sold them and recouped much of what I paid for them shortly after I stopped using them.

HIGH "ROLLERS"

My behavior as a compulsive shopper may seem frivolous, but if I resell my items shortly after I have extracted the value I derived from them, then it's not so profligate. You can no longer judge a book by its cover, no matter how shabby it is, nor an object by its price, no matter how expensive it is, nor a consumer by his tastes, no matter how lavish they are. The fact is that in the new auction culture, splurging on luxury items—whether they are grown-up toys or more serious acquisitions—will make good economic sense. So will buying the slightly used versions that come onto the secondary-goods market all the more often.

Take the case of one of the most carefully considered purchases many parents make: their first baby stroller. The earliest stroller was invented by a British garden architect for the third duke of Devonshire in 1733. Those early models were ornately decorated mini works of art, which were initially meant to be pulled by a goat. Only the upper class could afford them, but the practical benefits of the stroller were soon apparent and the industry democratized quickly. Today the stroller is a large part of a $6 billion baby-products industry in America, where expectant fathers blog about the latest models.

When the European Bugaboo Frog stroller reached America in 2001, it caused a stroller craze. The Frog appeared on television shows and dotted the pages of glossy magazines, where complacent celebrities—both male and female—could be found pushing their offspring along in the futuristic-looking stroller that retailed for more than $700. At least one enthusiastic buyer took the empty stroller for a proud test-drive around a grocery store even though his wife was still pregnant. Urban parents in particular sprung for the stroller, laying down money that they said would have otherwise gone into a second car, had they needed one.

The Bugaboo stroller—with its sporty and convertible X shape and tires that can handle grass, gravel, and sand—even made it into a museum. Elisabeth Agro, a curator at the Carnegie Museum of Art in Pittsburgh, put it in an exhibit on the material world of childhood, displaying the stroller alongside bright foam chairs from New Jersey. Agro told the *Pittsburgh Post-Gazette* that the stroller wasn't so much of an SUV in the stroller world as a Porsche.

And if Bugaboo is the Porsche of the stroller world, UK-based Silver Cross is the Rolls-Royce. Made of fine English leather, shiny lacquered steel with hand-sprung suspension, and hand-painted lining, this is the stroller brand preferred by the likes of Gwyneth Paltrow and Madonna. The Silver Cross Balmoral retails at a breathtaking $2,800.

At Kidville on Manhattan's Upper East Side, where a select group of parents ponies up hundreds to relax in spa style while their kids take Italian lessons and do yoga, this stroller is the new status symbol. The *New York Times* described the Kidville checkroom as a stroller lot. "Two dozen or more strollers were lined up in rows, Maclarens, Bugaboos, some Peg Peregos. High-tech strollers, strollers with attitude, strollers with sippie-cup holders. Stroller valets in headsets were moving the vehicles in and out." How far can the stroller craze go? Seriously, why pay hundreds or even thousands of dollars for a baby stroller?

Well, in the new auction culture, buying a high-end stroller will make a great deal of sense, not only because the product really is superior—sporting a stylish, youthful appearance, offering a more comfortable ride, and being more durable, and therefore safer for your child—but because the resale value will be superior, too. By extension, buying a used high-end stroller will also make good economic sense for those who can't or aren't quite willing to stretch for a new one. That's because even after a couple of years, the high-end model will probably still be a better-quality product than cheaper ones.

Several high-end stroller companies, including the Norwegian company Stokke, have intentionally made their products adjustable so they "grow" with children for a few years. Stokke spent five years developing the Xplory, which costs about $749 and has the look and feel of a Segway. Its tires are specially built to stay inflated forever. Frivolous? Consider this: the resale value on this kind of stroller will be higher because the people buying it in the secondary market will also be able to get more use out of it.

So take another look at those high-end strollers. They're not just some expensive status symbol or crazy fad. Buying one makes perfect sense. Granted, there are plastic strollers selling online for $12.99 that even come with pop-up shades made out of SPF 50 fabric. But how long is that lemon of a stroller going to last? Even the Buick of strollers will likely be relegated to the closet or Goodwill in several years. Buying a new stroller for $700 is a good deal. A liquid secondhand stroller market means that your child is safe and happy in a stroller that you're proud to push, and then, when the harness is too snug, you can sell it for about $550 on eBay. It will have cost you about the same as if you had bought a mediocre stroller to begin with. Even a black Silver Cross Balmoral goes for about $1,950 on eBay, saving one lucky parent hundreds of dollars.

Buying one of these strollers after a couple years of use is also a great deal, especially so if you then resell it when you're done. One of the most appealing—and also the most economically powerful—features of the new robust secondary-goods marketplace is that more consumers will be able to own the higher-quality goods because they can buy previously owned versions or get money back from selling them after a few years of use.

THE BEAUTY OF TRADING UP

Nothing beats that first rush of enthusiasm for something new and wonderful. The Pixar movie *Toy Story* became a hit by making us care about Woody and Jessie and the other toys that were no longer loved the way they were when the main character,

Andy, first held them. We identify with them because we understand what happened to them. It's human nature to be attracted to the latest thing. The trick is to accept that and incorporate it into our lives in a way that balances utility and value. More kids will get pleasure out of Woody and Jessie sooner. Mom will be less likely to view those toys as future attic dwellers.

With the strengthened secondary market, you will be able to "reach" more often for more expensive things, like the shiny Buzz Lightyear toy that Andy pined for in *Toy Story*. In general, the goods we would expect to have the highest resale value, and therefore the lowest cost of temporary ownership, are those of higher quality and desirability. Consequently, more people will be able to afford upscale products that they never could have managed before, as long as they expect to own them only temporarily and to resell them for a good return, or are happy buying them used. We'll all reach more and more, simply because we can.

Take a moment to think about your wish list. Now consider what it will actually cost you to own some of these items:

What's on Your Wish List?

Product	New**	Slightly Used*	Cost to Own
30-gigabyte iPod	$349	$225	$125
Hermès tie	$145	$86	$59
Montblanc pen	$285	$100	$185
Cartier Roadster watch	$4,600	$2,250	$2,350
Baccarat crystal bowl	$375	$205	$170
Schwinn spin bike	$700	$299	$401
Bugaboo stroller	$729	$548	$181

Recent eBay ending prices (average age of items sold: one to two years)
**Manufacturer's suggested retail*

Imagine that you have a hot date next week and want to impress.

Here's how it works to buy something you really like but can't bring yourself to spend the money on. Instead of walking into Bloomingdale's and spending $60 on a blah house brand tie, you can purchase a beautiful classic and unmistakable Hermès tie in the secondary market for $86 (the same tie retails for $145 plus tax in the store). Your date will never know you bought it on eBay, nor will the guys in the office the next morning. And if you get tired of it in the future, you are likely to get back most of the $86 you spent on it, less the dropshop's commission of $20 or $30. What a way to dress for success (and have extra money left over to pay for the date)!

Temporary ownership is an exciting new way of thinking about our connections to objects, a way of thinking that will empower us to enrich our lives by making purchases that we find more satisfying overall.

Embracing temporary ownership means just saying no to second best and letting yourself reach for the things that will thrill you the way your favorite birthday gifts did when you were a child or the way you feel when you go shopping for a new outfit or a new piece of technology. In this new culture, you can have that thrill over and over and over again, and have permission to do so—guilt free. When there's a good resale market, it just makes good economic sense to purchase high-value products with the intent to own them temporarily and then sell. The money you recoup when you turn in your expensive stroller, for example, can be put into a new bike for your child.

In the future, you won't have to be rich to buy an Hermès tie or a space-age stroller, just the way you don't have to be a millionaire to own a Mercedes today, unlike twenty-five or thirty years ago.

STAYING AHEAD OF THE CURVE

Another advantage of temporary ownership will be that at any given point in time we'll own newer goods. When we choose to own something for a defined period of time rather than for life, we most likely will purchase another, newer item to replace it when we sell the first one. Consequently, we will have made two other, different purchases during that period, rather than one, and will probably make even more purchases as we sell the second one and replace it with a third, and so on.

Advances in technology make it easy to want your possessions to be temporary because you know you'll want the next model when it arrives. Take cell phones, for example. No matter how fancy or high-tech a phone I buy, someone else has a better one a month (if not a week or even a few days) later. But in order to upgrade today, I have to pay full price for a new phone or sign up for a binding one- or two-year contract with the phone company, knowing that I'm not only locked in to a service plan that might not be optimal for me down the road, but also that I'm going to miss out on the new models of phones that the company puts out in the interim. But once there's a liquid secondary market for cell phones, I'll have a number of options and I'll be much less likely to have to pay the full price. I may decide that rather than buying a cell phone and using it until it breaks or becomes obsolete, I will own the phone for a few months, sell it, and then put the proceeds towards a newer phone model, effectively reducing the amount I'll have to pay for that new one.

Active secondary markets are also giving us an opportunity to consider temporarily owning products that we never considered for temporary ownership before. This temporary ownership amounts to a system similar to a lease, the cost of which will be driven primarily by a product's "residual value," meaning its fair market value at the end of the lease period. But unlike a traditional lease, where there is a predetermined end date, you will have the freedom to choose when you want the period of ownership to expire.

Think about the last time you bought a television. Chances are you didn't buy the newest, most expensive, top-of-the-line model, because even if you could afford it, you knew with certainty that there would be an even better top-of-the-line model out in a few months, and another one after that, and so on. So you probably bought the second- or third-best television with the expectation that you could trade up in a few years. You want to avoid feeling like you're overpaying for the status of being first on the block with the newest model once every two years. This pattern always leaves you behind the curve, even if it made some economic sense. But what if you could sign a long-term contract with Sony or Toshiba that would get you the newest models as they become available? Since you're never getting "outdated," you're much more inclined to pay top dollar. Toshiba and Sony will be able to offer this type of option since they will be able to predict the future value of their current models with accuracy, and they'll build that knowledge into their pricing plans. Rather than buying an actual product, you will be able to buy a product line, a contract giving you the right to seamlessly upgrade to a stream of future products as they are released.

SMART SELLING

Tapping into the potential of the secondary-goods market will require us to have a better understanding of what we buy. We'll need to know how the usefulness of our goods will change over time. It will also help to become familiar with how strong the marketplace is for certain items, if we choose to resell them. And we'll have to be prepared to buy goods more often, trading in our old versions for new ones instead of letting the boxes pile up in the closet. Anticipating this turnover will help us avoid wasting what we've got.

The point at which it makes sense to sell an item rather than hold it, as well as the expected cost of temporary ownership, will be different for each person and each product. This is because we all have our own tastes and preferences, so every person's utility curve for a given item will be different. When it comes to the utility of a gray suit, my taste may not be someone else's, and vice versa. Likewise, its value, as well its expected depreciation over time, will differ from brand to brand. The current and expected value of an Armani suit would differ from the value of a Hugo Boss or a no-name suit from a low-end department store. In addition, these values will change from time to time. Part of what affects these values is the nature of the product and its vulnerability to external factors such as appeal and durability. Consider that the latest, sleekest digital camera will become outdated faster than a classic Rolex watch. A pair of shoes will be more susceptible to a decline in value over time than a piece of platinum jewelry due to its natural tendency to wear and tear. Appeal can also be influenced by geography—for example, a Gottex bathing suit will be worth more in December in Uruguay than it would be in New York City.

The use that your own belongings have for you is a personal matter, but with respect to the likely future market price of the item, an active secondary market can provide some insight into how that product will hold its value over time. Take a look at what a one-year-old apple green iPod Mini goes for today compared to its original price and you get some idea of the price you may be able to get for your new iPod in a year's time. Determining exactly when to sell something you own today still involves guesswork—weighing the amount of use you get out of that suit relative to its possible resale value.

Figuring out when to sell sounds like it requires an algorithm that scientists would need to pore over for years under fluorescent lights. It won't be. In the future, thoughtful shoppers will be able to use various informational tools that can help determine an approximate time to trade. It will likely be as simple as glancing at a chart.

As for general rules about when to sell, it's helpful to consider the way the used-car market works. As soon as someone buys a car and drives it out of the dealer's lot, the car's value depreciates rapidly. In the first year after purchase, it's not unusual for a car's value to decline by upwards of 25 percent. The following year, the value will likely go down by less, perhaps 15 percent. In the years after that, the depreciation curve flattens and perhaps will decrease by 10 percent each year thereafter. Relatively speaking, the decline after the third year is constant. On an absolute basis, though, it's not. If you purchased a car that is worth $40,000 after three years, it will decline by 10 percent to be worth $36,000 in the fourth year, a decline of $4,000. In the fifth year, it will be worth $32,400, a decline of $3,600. In the sixth year, it will be worth $29,160, a decline of $3,240. As each year passes it costs you less and less to own it, making it easier to sell even as the utility continues to decline.

Ideally, you'll wait for about three years to sell your car. At that point, there is less depreciation and a lower cost of ownership in a period of declining utility. This is why leases are typically structured for at least three years. While this type of depreciation curve tends to make sense for cars, our personal items are more volatile. Accordingly, while one product or brand might be worth holding on to for three years before selling, another might be better sold in its second year. Take computers and shoes, for example. While both technology and fashion are evolving rapidly, your notebook will have greater utility in the outer years than your outdated shoes. In the future, whether it's a laptop or a trendy pair of shoes, we'll modify our behavior to sell at a time that takes our objectives into consideration and also balances value against our personal utility.

Right now, if you're considering purchasing a product and you want to estimate the cost of owning it for a period of time and then selling it, you will have to take an educated guess. You'll need to think about how the object's utility will change over time as well as what the object's market value will be over time. But the system will soon improve. When you want to find out what the best travel fares are, you turn to the travel section of a newspaper or you check an online search engine. The same goes for stock quotes. Eventually, consumers will be able to consult value tables for the most popular cell phones, shoes, designer labels, and other personal belongings. The value-table system will have a stock market feel to it—a way to look at the things you own and evaluate their worth. These tables will be available in newspapers and other publications. Online, trustworthy Web sites will post the values in real time so consumers can use the information to decide when and how to maximize a trade-up to a new model.

An informed buyer who decides to purchase a used portable digital music player like an iPod will know its exact long-term market value, and therefore will buy it at the right price today. Another consumer will be able to purchase—for a premium—the right to trade up his laptop computer for the next five years, at yearly intervals. Someone else will be able to see how the new cell phone model coming out will affect the value of last year's model.

As you, the consumer, learn the importance of residual value, you'll become accustomed to projecting an item's value a year or a decade into the future with help from value charts and other tools. For many people, these projections might sound awkward or beside the point. Why spoil the fun by thinking ahead to some diminished incarnation of the precious new television set you're considering buying? The answer is simple: because you can have even *more* fun and derive even more pleasure from buying a new television set if you give yourself more buying power when you accurately calculate its future value.

RESIDUAL THINKING

An accessible and liquid secondary market allows us to extract maximum value from the possessions we don't want. It will also encourage us to maintain the products we buy more carefully.

The ways in which we interact with our personal possessions today are a reflection of the generally limited view we take of their likely value in the future, and when that view becomes more expansive, our interaction with those things will change as well. When temporary ownership becomes a truly viable option, our

behavior will change in myriad ways. We will have different relationships to objects, and in most cases we'll be more attentive to
maintaining them. When you put on a pair of shoes that you know
you'll be wearing only for one night, or when you strap on a watch
you plan to wear for only six months, you'll be more conscious of
these possessions. Will you be more careful about how you throw
around your BlackBerry, knowing that if it's all scratched up, it
will sell for less?

The natural tendency will be to take more care, the way we
have with possessions that have sentimental value. In the past,
you didn't just leave your great-grandmother's porcelain cups lying around within the reach of small children. You wanted them
to be in pristine condition and in the family forever, so you were
very gentle with them. But with a pair of shoes, up until now you
really didn't think too much about them. You likely thought
about them the same way you thought about an umbrella—
useful, possibly nice looking, but ultimately there to serve a purpose. Your mind-set will change when you start caring for things
with the hope that someone else will want to own them in the
near future. You'll ensure that those shoes are in a good condition. You'll be gentler with small electronic devices. And being
careful will actually pay off.

In order for this cycle to take full effect and work to our advantage, we need to reach a new comfort level with buying used
goods. Learning to take care of the belongings we expect to own
temporarily raises the question: aren't there some people who
will never want to shop for used goods? After all, buying more
expensive items than we would have otherwise bought hinges on
our confidence in being able to sell them later for a good price. So
will the market for them hold up?

LEARNING TO LOVE THE PRE-OWNED

There will always be some people who opt to avoid the secondary markets, but eBay's success demonstrates that millions of people have already changed the way they think about used goods. Let's not forget that the number of eBay users has grown to more than 150 million people worldwide. It's already the type of marketplace where thirteen CDs sell every minute and eight video games sell every second, and it's not hard to understand that leap from a mind-set where renting a videotape is perfectly acceptable behavior to one where buying it used is equally appropriate is a pretty small one. Cars, computers, consumer electronics, music, books, and movies top the eBay charts as most frequently traded. Below is a recent "hot list" from eBay data showing the most traded goods in a given day:

Hot List (August 5, 2005)

1. Event tickets
2. Cell phones
3. Wristwatches
4. Handbags
5. Men's shoes
6. Women's shoes
7. Video game systems
8. Apple Powerbook notebooks
9. Fiction books
10. Magazine back issues
11. Diamond earrings
12. Electric guitars

This list gives you a glimpse of the breadth of the auction culture. It has already happened in the car market and the sporting goods market and is well under way in the music business. Buying used CDs quickly became a widely accepted way to access music, and now it hardly matters whose initials are inked onto the CD itself when so many of us are transferring the music we own from disc to MP3 players. CDs are one thing, but what happens when we want to make sure a pair of shoes or a suit is in an ideal condition for resale? Based on what I know about the secondary marketplace, one of the ways the market will grow involves the entry of more and more specialists who will get our pre-owned goods into the best shape for selling (more on that later).

The hottest brand-name items, especially in luxury goods, will make up the leading edge of growth in the resale market. This is actually one of the reasons why I helped to found Portero. In the wake of how important luxury goods have become to the secondary marketplace, one looming question about the growth of this market is: won't manufacturers, especially the leading-brand companies, suffer from the growth of the resale of their goods? Isn't it inevitable that these companies will take a big hit when so many people begin buying used versions of their goods? Actually, a liquid secondary market where possessions are in constant movement will have a positive effect on the primary market. As we'll see in the next chapter, companies that stay ahead of the curve will be profiting from the new paradigm.

6 FOR THE GOOD OF ALL
The Net Effect

If we all begin to adopt the auction culture and start trading up to brands we'd prefer, won't that put a damper on new product sales for many of the companies that produce these products? Not at all. Luxury brands have grown so popular in online auctions that the purveyors of these brands have been leading the charge against the growth of the online secondary-goods market. These companies have become extremely creative in coming up with ways to keep their products from being traded. Instead, they should have more confidence in the value of their products and the power of sales in the secondary market to boost their business. Just consider the case of the Birkin bag.

Besides celebrity and notoriety, Lil' Kim and Martha Stewart don't seem to have a tremendous amount in common, but one taste that they both share is for a very special type of handbag named for a waifish British actress whose life has been filled with its own share of controversy.

London-born Jane Birkin made her film debut with a small part in Richard Lester's 1965 romp *The Knack*. Soon thereafter she was, quite appropriately, Exquisite Thing in the otherwise forgettable 1966 Warren Beatty vehicle, *Kaleidoscope*. But it was her role the following year as a naked and giggling teenager in Michelangelo Antonioni's cult classic film *Blow-Up* that solidified her celebrity status.

The photographer Cecil Beaton called young Birkin "the most beautiful woman in England." *Time* magazine described her as "a swinger in the Bond mold," but then dismissed her as an accessory for her husband, James Bond theme composer John Barry. Birkin quickly deaccessorized herself and moved to Paris, where she would go on to record the suggestive "*Je t'aime . . . moi non plus*" with French bad boy Serge Gainsbourg. The song quickly climbed to number one on the UK charts, thanks to the widespread furor over Birkin's sighing, attention-getting interpretation, described by *W* magazine as a "famously suggestive ode to sex." The BBC banned the song and the Vatican denounced it, and Birkin's edgy reputation was solidified. Jane Birkin would go on to act in more than fifty films, sing on fourteen albums, and become a knight of the British Empire for her services to acting. Her name, however, is most often associated with a different kind of artistry—one that began with a chance encounter.

In the early 1980s, Birkin was boarding the Concorde carrying a bag made by the French fashion house Hermès.

"My stuff kept falling out of the one I had," Birkin told the writer Harriet Welty Rochefort in an interview in *Paris Kiosque*. "As I was boarding the Concorde, a gentleman watching me said, 'What a mess!' I replied that I loved the bag, but it needed pockets.

"The man said, 'I'll do it.'"

The man turned out to be Jean-Louis Dumas, chairman of Hermès, and he meant what he said. In 1984, Hermès debuted a new model handbag—a roomy tote with a thirty-five-centimeter diameter, strong and delicately shaped handles, two interior pockets (one with zipper), and a three-piece clasp. Dumas named it for its inspiration.

By the time the Birkin made its debut, Hermès had spent nearly a century and a half building a reputation as one of the finest manufacturers of luxury goods in the world. The fashion house originated with Dumas' great-grandfather Thierry Hermès, who made leather harnesses and equestrian accessories for an exclusive clientele that included European royal families. Since then, the business had steadily expanded into the consumer retail sector. In 1923, Hermès used its reputation for quality materials and exquisite craftsmanship to start making handbags, introducing the first women's model, the Bolide, which sported a freshly patented zipper. The fashion house's Haut à Courroies bags were large enough to carry riding boots. In the 1930s, Hermès introduced its famous scarves and began producing a calfskin model purse, stitched by hand in Paris and finished off with melted beeswax.

Hermès's breakthrough into the superluxury-goods market came when a pregnant Princess Grace appeared in *Life* magazine in 1956 holding up an Hermès bag to demurely cover her bulging stomach. It immediately became known as the Kelly bag, a brand name connoting their shared elegance and quality and suggestive of the desirability the model went on to achieve. No doubt it was the popularity of the Kelly bag that inspired Dumas to name his more current model for Jane Birkin, but it is unlikely that even he could have hoped for the success that would follow.

Birkins are gorgeous things, and of preeminent quality. Dumas himself told the *Montreal Gazette* that it takes eighteen hours to hand-construct each piece and that craftspeople undergo five years of training before they can begin stitching the bags together. Defective bags are shredded and employees are only allowed to make and keep their own specially identified bags once every year.

But it is the exclusivity of owning a Birkin that gives the bag its transcendent aura. Within a decade of its arrival on the market thousands of women around the world put their names on waiting lists for the privilege of decorating their arms with a Birkin. Today, Birkins come in a dizzying array of sizes, colors, linings, leathers, and skins. There's even an entire book of sample materials from which potential owners can choose. The retail prices start in the $5,000 range and go straight up from there. (A smaller crocodile version comes in four colors, has gold hardware, and is detailed with diamonds—*Vogue* even featured the bag, priced at $75,300, in 2004.) And they're still not available. As London's Sunday *Independent* reported in September 2004, "There is a waiting list to get on the waiting list, which is itself two and a half years long."

Would-be carriers and collectors have tirelessly scoured consignment shops and scavenged estate sales in pursuit of these rare treasures for years, so what happened when the Birkin bag met eBay, where fifteen handbags and other accessories sell every minute? Does Hermès, a fashion house that has built a cult following by making the bag hard to obtain, lose out when the secondary market becomes awash in used Birkins?

Absolutely not. Birkins, like many high-end luxury items, actually retain their value or exceed their retail prices on the secondary market, which creates even more demand for the glamorously utilitarian handbags. The waiting list is longer than ever.

THE GAME YOU'VE GOT TO HAVE

Exclusive luxury items aren't the only goods for which the secondary market has been shown not only to have no corrosive effect on retail sales but to actually offer manufacturers some benefits.

The ultramodern handheld Nintendo DS video gaming console has two screens for different perspectives on the action, touch screen capability, voice recognition software, and built-in wireless communication so gamers can compete against someone in the same room or someone on the other side of the globe. "In DS games, you can move sailboats around with your breath, push game characters with your finger and play wirelessly with other DS-toting friends who don't even own the same games," the *Rocky Mountain News* reported shortly after the gadget's debut in 2004. When the reviews came back, the console was frequently called "the funnest." Originally, Nintendo shipped only one million of them to North American retailers in late November 2004, but in the course of a few weeks, it was clear that more were needed. Many more. Nearly every retailer in the country was sold out. Nintendo DS gaming consoles began selling on eBay for almost double their $149.99 retail price— and as holiday deadlines neared, they were snatched up by desperate parents as quickly as they were offered.

Nintendo eventually did respond to the increased demand, shipping 400,000 more of the sought-after consoles. As a result, the price on eBay fell, but not to levels you would expect. Consoles bundled with extra games and accessories are still moving through eBay at close to retail price, with some sellers continuing to unload them for more.

In the gaming space, there's always something sleeker on the horizon as manufacturers continually push the limits of technology. In March 2005, Sony debuted its first handheld portable version of the PlayStation 2, which contained technologically enhanced features. Though the company tried to step lightly in the balancing act between overproducing and underdelivering and produce just enough units to satisfy demand (while still watching over profits by keeping manufacturing costs down), actual demand surpassed expectations. The *Chicago Sun-Times* reported long lines outside electronics stores that stocked it. Predictably, eBay sales of the PlayStation 2 took off and the device sold there for nearly $100 more than the retail price. Hours afterwards, one twenty-five-year-old who bought a portable PlayStation 2 told the *Sun-Times* that if it turns out he doesn't like it, he'll just sell it on eBay.

It sounds like retailers are getting the short end of the stick, right? Actually, this type of resale behavior doesn't really affect retailers at all. Many of the people who line up at a store hours before it opens on the day of a new toy release are similar to scalpers who buy sports or concert tickets with the intention to resell them at a higher price. What drives the market is the difference between the value the seller places on his time as he waits on line for hours to buy a game console for resale, and the value the buyer (or his parents in this case) places on his time.

Take the case of Brian, a sixteen-year-old high school student who is more than happy to wait in line at a store for three hours to buy the new $150 Nintendo DS gaming system. The store limits each customer to one unit because of the enormous demand, but Brian isn't buying for himself—he feels confident he can sell it on eBay for $300, leaving him a profit of $150. Assuming he spends two hours in the auction process to sell the item, he has invested five hours to make $150. This enterprising sixteen-year-old is making $30 per hour for his time—or more than $60,000 per year, if he could do this eight hours a day for five days a week.

On the other side of the transaction is Jonathan, whose nine-year-old son has been asking for the new Nintendo system for his birthday. Jonathan is a successful orthopedic surgeon whose annual income of more than $500,000 places a $250-per-hour value on his time. Jonathan is delighted that he only has to click once on eBay to buy his son, Jason, his new toy. Had he waited on line for the privilege of paying retail, he would have saved $150 in cash, but paid a theoretical $750 in lost time value. So everybody comes out a winner in this transaction. Jonathan wins by saving $600, Brian wins by making $150 and Jason wins by receiving the instant gratification of being one of the first kids at school to have the hot new game system.

The retailer also wins. It has the exact same experience it would have had without the secondary transaction. It would have sold the exact same quantity of units with or without the scalpers (remember, there was limited supply) because while retailers could charge more in the first place for their products when demand is high and supply is scarce, they don't for fear of creating bad will with their customers and, in many cases, to protect their flow of product from the manufacturers, who frown upon price gouging.

A closer look at the situation reveals that manufacturers actually benefit from the profiteers trading in their goods. By releasing too few units into the primary market, the manufacturers create a frenzy as gamers clamor to secure scarce items. However, if stock of their favorite brand is out, they may lose their patience and migrate to an alternative brand that is more readily available. Once that occurs, the original brand not only loses that sale but a stream of future sales as the customer adopts the new brand. With Jason's birthday coming in a week and the DS nowhere to be found, his desperate father may have decided that the new X box was an acceptable substitute, and once he had the opportunity to play it, Jason might have agreed. Think of how many Nintendo customers were saved by eBay traders coming to their rescue.

Okay, you might say, I can buy that the resale market is a good thing for companies when their goods are in short supply, but that's not always the case. Aren't the Birkin bag and the latest hot video game product extreme examples? Who, retailers might ask in a panicky voice, is going to buy a Louis Vuitton handbag at Bloomingdale's or a Callaway driver from the local boutique golf shop when the same ones are available on exchanges like eBay for a lower price? While the intuitive answer seems to be "no one," it's actually not. A robust secondary market will actually be great for the primary-goods market for leading-brand products in general—for Louis Vuitton and Callaway, and for Bloomingdale's and the golf shops—just like the explosion in used-car sales had a positive impact on the market for new cars. Consider Mercedes. Its certified pre-owned car program made it possible for more people to drive out of the lot with one. Over the past ten years, the company's sales have more than tripled. Its sales figures for 2004 marked the highest sales volume in the car company's history.

THE BRAND-BUILDING BOOM

Now let's look at how the same logic plays out in general for leading brand-name products. My friend Charlotte is a consumer who has embraced the auction culture lifestyle. One day she decided to sell a classic monogrammed Louis Vuitton sixty-inch Keepall 60 duffle bag that she had bought the previous year for $820. It's still a great bag, but after using it for a while, she longed for the special edition, multicolored, Murakami-designed handbag version. She wanted to feel the rush of the shopping experience, and to update her look with the latest style. She's a die-hard LV junkie and just can't help herself, but she also knew she couldn't afford to buy a new bag if she didn't recoup at least some of the value of her old one. So Charlotte headed over to a local dropshop with her classic bag, and a few days later it appeared on eBay.

Charlotte's classic duffle sold for $560. After fees and commissions to both eBay and the dropshop, she pocketed a cool $400 to put towards her new purchase. She was thrilled because, in the end, the bag cost her only $420 (the $820 she originally paid less the $400 she recouped) to sport during the past year—less than one dollar a day—and suddenly she had the cash to shop for the next one.

Now consider the continuing life of the Keepall bag Charlotte sold. Most likely, the purchaser was a similar young woman, one who frequently shops on eBay because she adores fashion and loves deals. She probably competed with about ten other bidders in a heavily contested auction to win the bag. When she started carrying her new bag around and showing it off, she probably told her friends about how she bought it. "Not only was it authentic LV and a bargain," she might say to them, "look what fantastic condition it is in." Chances are eBay had eight new fashionistas searching for bags on their site the next week, causing an increased demand on a somewhat limited supply of bags. LV's brand value went up that week as eight more people stopped to think of one of their products.

This scenario is quite pervasive, as backed up by the historical data for Louis Vuitton on eBay. The term "Louis Vuitton" became the second-most searched term on eBay in 2004, indicating that the secondary market is stimulating people to think of its brand—a lot! Not surprisingly, prices have increased over time as more and more people are searching for their products and competing for the goods. Take the case of that Keepall bag Charlotte sold. Two months later, a bag identical to Charlotte's $560 bag sold for $620. Meanwhile, the sales for new Louis Vuitton products have experienced double-digit growth as recently reported in the company's annual report.

TIPPING THE SCALES

One of the most counterintuitive features of the secondary-goods revolution is that the sale of used goods, even the only slightly used versions, will generally not only not undermine the sale of the new products for most goods, it may actually boost those sales. There will always, after all, be a real and appreciable difference between buying something new and getting it used, no matter how close to mint condition the used item is. That's why prices for used items generally have an upper limit and why we can expect that a robust secondary market will push certain consumers even more fervently toward new products.

The new market always keeps the previously owned market in check. At some point, assuming that a particular LV bag, for example, is readily available in department stores or boutiques, the price of a used Louis Vuitton bag can't go any higher. In other words, the secondary-market price will reach a point where the trade-off between buying the same bag new and bidding on a used one no longer makes sense. I call this point the secondary-market equilibrium. No savvy consumer is going to pay the retail price on eBay when he or she can just get the bag brand-spanking-new from a local department store or boutique (unless, of course, you can't get it new—like a Birkin).

Think of the market for cars again. In any stable market where there is abundant supply, where you can go to any dealer and get the exact model and color you want right off the lot, a used car will always sell for a significant amount less than its new counterpart, even when there's no discernible wear and tear. We banter about our fondness for that new-car smell, and while we tend to be (mostly) kidding, there are always people (myself included) who psychologically value the knowledge that we were the first to ever own, drive, wear, live in, use, et cetera, the things that we bring home.

Those people will continue to be perfectly willing to pay a premium for new versions of many items they buy. Many will never leave the primary market, at least not for certain goods, because when it comes to certain items there is no reasonable price at which they are willing to make a trade-off and buy those goods pre-owned or in an online exchange. After all, a good deal more than just the purchased item comes along with buying something new. For one thing, there's the shopping experience itself. For some people, shopping is a social activity: getting together with the girls to spend the day at Bloomies. For others, it's just the opposite: a time when you can isolate yourself from the world and indulge alone, transporting yourself away from the grind of everyday life. And for some, it's a momentous event because the object purchased has a special sentimental value, like going with your spouse to a fancy jeweler or watch store to pick out a time-piece for his fortieth birthday. These experiences can never be duplicated in an online exchange, and to the extent you place value on them, the benefit you receive in a lower price will never make up for the loss of that experience.

For luxury goods, a large part of what the market offers is simply experience: the beautifully decorated store, the white-glove service, and the dainty boxes and sleek bags that guard and help transport your new purchases home are all part of the experience. And you pay for it. The experience of shopping in a fancy store can't be duplicated online, at least not today, and that helps reinforce the value that a retailer delivers as part of the purchase price. In addition, the boutiques offer early access to the newest models, and those who can afford to buy those models new will always appreciate the value of doing so.

THE PSYCHOLOGY OF THE NEW

There are certain items some people will never buy secondhand, and those things will be different for everyone. For example, I don't think I personally would ever buy a pre-owned mattress as my primary mattress. Sure, I'll sleep on a used mattress—we all do when we stay at hotels. Even the finest room in the most ex-pensive hotel in the world isn't going to offer its clients new mat-tresses each time they stay. So, why don't I buy a used mattress if

I could do so more cheaply than I could buy a new one? It's psychological. I sleep on my mattress at home every night, so if I sleep an average of seven hours a night, I will spend almost 30 percent of my life on my mattress. Knowing this, I decided to buy a Duxiana, a Swedish mattress that is considered by many to be the Rolls-Royce of mattresses. Duxiana was still a relatively small company little known to Americans in 1998, when my decorator introduced me to their mattress "sleeping system." I had said I wanted the best bed money could buy, so she walked me into the Duxiana store in Manhattan. I left with a mattress that put me back $7,500, and seven years later I think of it as one of the best investments I have ever made.

The warranty on my Duxiana says it should last at least twenty years, which equates to around 7,300 nights, or "uses." Having spent more than $7,500 for the mattress, that's about a dollar per night for the life of the mattress. And that's assuming it will have no resale value after the warranty is up. I'm happy spending a dollar a night knowing that I was the first person to sleep on it the day I brought it home and that it had 7,299 uses left in it when I woke up the next morning.

Despite their reputation for quality, comfort, and durability, Duxiana mattresses currently don't have a strong value in the secondary market—at least not online. In the last 120 days, only $15,000 worth of Duxiana mattresses were traded at an average value of around $1,500 per mattress. That's ten mattresses sold in three months (compared to more than 30,000 other mattresses sold on eBay for more than $3 million during the same period of time). Each mattress is also selling on average for $6,000 less than what I paid for the same mattress new.

As I've discussed, I wouldn't buy a used mattress—even a

Duxiana—as my primary mattress, but I can imagine circumstances where I would spring for it. I could get one for my vacation home. I only spend fifty nights a year there, so buying a new Duxiana for it feels frivolous to me. The reduced use means I would have to spend about $8 per night to own it over the same period of time—eight times the price of the same mattress I have at home, which costs me a dollar per night. But if I could buy it slightly used with roughly the same life expectancy for $1,500, it would cost me around $1.50 per night to sleep on it for the thousand nights I plan to spend in my beach home over the next twenty years.

When I buy a used Duxiana, the primary market doesn't lose out. I would never have bought my primary mattress used on eBay, so Duxiana would never have lost me as a customer in the first place. Furthermore, without the secondary market, I would never have even pondered the value of a used Duxiana and then bought one for my vacation home.

The future makeup of buyers in the secondary market will likely break down into the same tiers we see today in the primary market—the elite who buy luxury brands, those who buy a combination of leading brand-name items and bargain brands, those who are always bargain hunting, and shoppers in economic trouble who can barely afford what they need. As the secondary market develops, these basic categories probably won't change. The rise of auction culture will, however, allow more of us to get our hands on better brands. Many of us will become hybrid buyers, preferring to continue buying some items new while at the same time buying plenty of other items used from online sites.

What will happen to nonluxury, non-name-brand items? As auction culture evolves, there will be less of a market for lower-end to middle-market brands. People will largely migrate to either better brands or take the notion of temporary ownership to the opposite extreme and seek goods they know they will be disposing after a period of time. Those that reach for better products will recognize that because those products have enough residual value they can be resold at some point in the future. Others will buy brands of lesser stature, knowing they will be disposed of, since there will be no market for them in the future.

BRAND MANAGEMENT

The online secondary market actually may have boosted sales for Vuitton through increased brand recognition and product availability. EBay certainly hasn't hurt what is widely considered the most profitable luxury brand on the planet, as sales for LV grew by 16 percent in 2003 to $3.8 billion according to a 2004 *Business-Week* article. It grew at a similar rate in 2004. With its growth in recent years, approximately $50 million of Louis Vuitton products currently trade on eBay's U.S. exchange annually. These goods currently fetch an average of 50 percent of their retail value, which indicates that at least 2 percent of Louis Vuitton's $3.8 billion in goods seem to be resold annually.* Remember the multicolored Murakami handbag Charlotte wanted so much that she decided to sell her classic LV Keepall 60 duffle bag? Louis Vuitton generated more than $300 million in sales of Murakami products in 2003. So, Charlotte's new bag is at least one Murakami-designed handbag purchased at an LV store for around $1,300 that wouldn't

---

*The actual number is close to $100 million in retail value

have been bought if it wasn't for eBay. And Murakami-designed leather products represented almost 10 percent of the nearly $50 million in LV sales on eBay last year, while the primary market for the new bags also boomed.

The conclusions from these various points of data are necessarily extrapolated. If we continue with this logic one can further extrapolate that at least two out of every one hundred bags Vuitton makes are sold on eBay annually, and if trends show us that a healthy Louis Vuitton manages its brand well, the growth of auction culture can benefit the company even more. As customers like my friend Charlotte replace their bags with new ones, making their recently used ones available to be owned and adored by people for whom LV was once only a dream, LV begins to build a foundation of customer adoption much earlier in the lives of their prospective customers. Now fashion- and budget-conscious consumers can live the LV lifestyle before they have the disposable income to fully support it, and they'll be well-indoctrinated customers when they can finally combine ownership with the experience of buying a bag in an LV store. And as one prospective customer buys up, the company simultaneously improves the breadth, presence, and value of their brand in coming years with her contemporaries, her "audience." And none of this will negatively affect their sales in the primary market, just like the availability of used Mercedeses didn't detract from sales of their new cars. Both Mercedes and Louis Vuitton made highly successful products before the secondary markets kicked in. In fact, the strength of their products in the secondary market and their accessibility to the upwardly-but-not-yet-there mobile is what seeded their success.

SATURATION POINT

Despite the tangible and direct benefits, some brand owners have reacted to the advent of the secondary market in ways designed to prevent their products' resalability. Some companies have sued; others have ruthlessly shut down any auction online that even mentions their names. To some extent it's understandable—change is frightening. But the legacy of the damage done to a brand's value by overextension and by the influx of counterfeit products probably account for much of this trepidation.

"Remember," brand managers will caution, "the death of a luxury brand usually follows its overmining." By this they would mean the rapid overextension of a brand name whose sudden broad availability changes a fundamental value of the brand, thereby depleting the brand of much of its value in the process. That typically happens when the brand owner becomes greedy and opts to expand the supply of its products and to increase its available distribution channels so it can maximize its profits in the short run. But by oversupplying the market, it drives its prices down. And when the consumers of that brand see the market flooded with the designer products they used to snap up, they no longer feel special owning them. The brand loses its value, and to stay ahead of the masses, the brand's former customers migrate to a different brand.

The history of the prominent Lacoste brand depicts this and has come to serve as a brand-management cautionary tale. In 1927, Jean René Lacoste, a French tennis champion, was nicknamed Le Crocodile by the American press after supposedly betting on a match where the loser would buy the winner a suitcase made from alligator skin. Lacoste lost, refused to buy the bag, and from then on his teammates called him Le Crocodile. In jest, an artist friend of Lacoste, Robert George, drew the crocodile icon and Lacoste had it embroidered onto a blazer. When he retired from tennis, Lacoste decided to market his shirt with what had become a famous emblem. He founded La Société Chemise Lacoste to manufacture his shirts, and they were introduced to the public in 1933 in France.

Fashion historians believe the crocodile emblem—widely misidentified as an alligator—was the first instance of a designer logo to appear on a garment. Regardless, it became stunningly popular. The shirts reached the U.S. marketplace in 1952, and President Eisenhower quickly began wearing the shirt for his highly publicized golf games. By the 1970s, Lacoste had become the staple for preppy wear in the United States, and during its zenith from the 1970s to the early 1980s Lacoste raked in $400 million in U.S. sales alone. Everyone who was "anyone" packed their crocodile shirts to wear and be seen on holiday trips. Celebrities and sportsmen alike chose Lacoste for their casual sportswear, and the brand's popularity soared.

When General Mills, a multibillion-dollar food conglomerate, decided to get into the apparel industry in 1975, Lacoste was one of the first labels it targeted for acquisition. But they would soon find that they couldn't apply the same rules to the designer clothing business as they had to foodstuffs. Stanley Greenstein, Lacoste's CFO in the 1980s, remembers how aggressively General Mills looked to monetize the franchise by extending the brand to everything it could. "The alligator [or crocodile] logo became as commonplace as the cereals produced by General Mills [think Cheerios and Cocoa Puffs], as they put the logo on everything from eyeglasses to perfume to lingerie," he told me. But ubiquity wasn't kind to the alligator. "As the brand became mainstream, Lacoste no longer had the aspirational cachet that it once enjoyed," Greenstein said.

General Mills moved manufacturing from France to Hong Kong and America. The result was a striped and synthetic product of drastically inferior quality. The old Lacoste collars were made of cotton strong enough to be straightened; the new shirt collars flopped. Ralph Lauren and other brands quickly stepped into the void General Mills had created and successfully marketed their own preppy cotton to Lacoste's former high-end customer base.

In the early 1990s, the Lacoste family decided to regain control of the battered brand just a few years before René Lacoste passed away. The family was eager to reinvigorate the brand and paid $30 million to buy the American license back. The Lacoste family brought in fashion designer Christophe Lemaire as Lacoste's creative director in 2000, signaling a sea change for the brand. He introduced a rainbow of fresher colors to the shirt palate and made fitted shirts that appealed to women. There are signs that Lacoste is making a comeback. According to its site, the company sells forty-two million items per year now, which includes several clothing lines and a variety of sporting equipment and accessories. A three-ounce Lacoste Pour Femme perfume spray with the famous logo on it retails for $60 in the United States. Trendy New Yorkers have been seen sporting stretchy shirts with the tiny crocodile logo; Bloomingdale's started selling a women's Lacoste white cotton stretch T-shirt for $98, and the *Tampa Tribune* reported that teenagers there had put Lacoste shirts on their "in" list for 2005. But the brand still has a way to go. The shirts are trading rampantly on eBay for as little as $10 per shirt.

As for counterfeiters, Louis Vuitton, Hermès, Gucci, Chanel, and others have good reason to fight them to the death. When the market is flooded with cheap knockoff versions of original products, the damage to a brand can be immeasurable. Hermès recently cracked down on rubber versions of its famed Birkin, even when they were crafted as a satirical expression with seemingly good intentions. The fakes industry has exploded. The Counterfeiting Intelligence Bureau, an arm of the UK-based International Chamber of Commerce, reports that counterfeiting sets back the global economy by at least $350 billion a year. And according to the comptroller's estimates, counterfeits in New York City alone cost the city at least $1 billion in revenue in 2004. The more fakes there are, the more it appears that everyone has the real thing. When everyone appears to have one, those luxury-brand images suffer. The brand's prestige is diluted.

But on the other hand, the consumers who truly love brands are typically not the same consumers who support the underground counterfeit market. There is still no replacement for the real deal. A fake Birkin isn't going to last like a real one will, and if the fashion police don't notice, the real police just might. Customs agents seize fakes all the time, and while it may not be against the law to buy them, it is illegal to make or sell them. On the surface, this may seem like a good argument for the brand owners to be that much more concerned about the secondary-goods markets; after all they are peddling "real" products. But the opposite is true. Many of the purchasers of the real products being bought online might have bought a high-quality knockoff otherwise, especially given how hard it can be to tell these days that some knockoffs are fake. With sales of the real thing online, a company is extending its customer base while also maintaining the integrity of its product.

With the right brand management, the masses' ability to acquire luxury products secondhand will not destroy Louis Vuitton or Hermès or Chanel or any other brand that continues to control its product distribution in the primary market. Savvy luxury aficionados will appreciate the fact that the items they buy retain value, and they will attribute the great feeling of receiving a check for their previous possessions to the brand itself. The same thing happens when you sell your car for a good price after using it for a few years. You continue to feel good about having bought the brand—whether it's Mercedes, BMW, or Honda.

One advantage that auction culture holds for leading brands is that they will have access to a stronger market for new versions of their products. They'll find increasing demand for more frequent introductions of new items, both for the replenishment of the goods their customers decide to sell and also to ensure that their premier clients will be able to continue distinguishing themselves by the things they own. Mrs. Park Avenue will never want to own the same handbag that Average Jane now carries or be seen in the same dress as Ms. Main Street is now able to wear. So the luxury goods sector will have that much more opportunity to create new products for Mrs. Park Avenue that allow her to indulge her desire for exclusivity with more expensive new styles. Mrs. Park Avenue will still be able to feel special buying the brands she loves.

Another advantage for brands is that they will experience a surge from impulse spending. No longer will customers have to ponder at length about a purchase, thinking that they will be stuck with a product if down the line they realize they made the wrong decision. In the new auction culture people will spend more freely and shop more impulsively, knowing that the cost of poor purchasing decisions will not be great since they can always resell an item for good value and recoup a large portion of the original purchase price.

Brand owners have more control over what happens in the secondary market than they may realize. It's true that when a customer leaves an LV store with a beautiful handbag the company can't tell its customer what she can and can't do with the bag. Nevertheless, the company can influence what the item is worth in the secondary market, therefore controlling how it is sold. Product pricing in the primary market has a major influence on the secondary-market price. For example, if a bag today is selling for $500 retail and for $400 slightly used on eBay, and the manufacturer wants less of its product sold on eBay, all it has to do is push down the primary market price. When the price on the primary market goes down to $400, the product likely won't sell for that price on eBay because it will only sell there for less than retail (without taking supply and convenience into consideration). Sellers, discouraged by a lower price, might decide to continue owning the bag instead of selling it for such a low price. This behavior is quite common in the car market when manufacturers release subsequent-year car models without an increase in price. It softens pricing in the secondary market for the prior-year models and discourages people from selling their used cars.

Rather than the secondary market's undermining the primary, the two markets will work in unison, supporting each other. Not all businesses understand this yet, and, for sure, understanding how to deal with the secondary market as it booms will be challenging and require savvy analysis. As of now, some companies are embracing it while others are fighting it. One thing is clear, however: there is no turning back. The auction culture is progressing quickly and increasing numbers of companies—whether your company is a global behemoth or a small-town shop—will need to respond.

7 TO FIGHT OR NOT TO FIGHT

Corporate Responses to Change

My friend Howard Levitt drove toward the Midtown Tunnel in New York City on his way home from work one evening. He was sitting in his car at a stoplight along Third Avenue when the two men inside the next car over, a Navigator SUV, motioned for Howard to roll down his window so they could talk to him. Howard thought it might be entertaining to humor them.

"Hey, you wanna buy a Rolex?" one of the men called out as soon as Howard rolled down his window.

"Naaaah," Howard said.

"It's a real Rolex," the man insisted.

Howard glanced over quickly, then back at the light, which was still red.

"How do I know it's real?" he asked the man.

"It's from Tourneau," the man said proudly, as if that would end all discussion of the matter.

"What do you mean, 'It's from Tourneau'?" Howard asked him.

The light was still red, the column of cars was unmoving, and the fellow in the Navigator now had Howard's attention.

"I have the receipt," the man said. Howard now caught a glimpse of the unmistakable green Rolex box in the driver's hand.

"Let me see it," Howard shot back.

The sheet of paper poked out of the window almost immediately. Howard took it and the watch and studied both.

You could say Howard is a bit of a watch expert. The first thing he did with the watch was get a sense of how much it weighed, since less sophisticated fakes often do not have the right heft. But this watch had the right weight and the right heft. Next Howard looked for the Rolex crown on the inside of the bracelet, which was often missing on fakes. It was there.

Getting more involved now, he studied the small screws in the removable links of the bracelet—these, too, are often the wrong size, a telltale sign of a fake.

"Not bad," Howard was thinking to himself. "The screws are right."

Traffic was still going nowhere, and Howard was not about to give up easily. He kept looking and, finally, there it was: the bezel—the ring around the watch that holds in the glass. Once he noticed it, there was no mistaking it: the bezel was the wrong color. The counterfeiters had used the wrong kind of bezel.

Now his attention turned to the receipt. It looked like a real credit card receipt. That part checked out fine. But according to the receipt, the watch had been purchased at a place called Tourneau's. At first Howard assumed that was a dumb mistake—

who would misspell the name of the world's largest watch re-tailer, a store so well known to so many?

"That's a pretty good fake," Howard said as he handed the watch back to the man.

"It's not a fake," the man said.

"It's a fake," Howard repeated, his voice calm and assured.

"It's *not* a fake," the man insisted. "It's real."

The man kept up his pretense with such dogged effort that it amused Howard, so he decided to play along a little further.

"Why would you buy a watch when it's a fake?" he started to ask.

"It's a stolen credit card," the man explained.

That was a good line. It might have satisfied a lot of people, but not Howard Levitt.

"Guys, I hate to tell you this," Howard told the two men in the Navigator, "but you went through a lot of trouble with that stolen credit card because this is a fake watch."

Cars were now starting to move in front, and it was almost time for Howard to get rolling toward the Midtown Tunnel and home.

"It's *not* a fake," the man said. "We got it at Tourneau."

"Well, if you got it at Tourneau, they sold you a fake watch," Howard said.

By then the driver's poker face was gone. He could not hold back a smile.

"How do you know it's a fake?" the man finally had to ask, his cool confidence gone.

Howard put his car into gear.

"I'm the president of Tourneau," he said and pulled away, leaving the two men at the light.

.   .   .

HOWARD ISN'T THE only business executive concerned with spotting fakes. Counterfeiting has become a huge problem for leading
brands. Blatant offenders: a fake Kate Spade bag with a Burberry
design, a real Louis Vuitton gift bag that comes with a counterfeit
purse, and a badly made (i.e., blurry and obviously Photo-
shopped) copy of a Pokémon board game. Counterfeiting high-
end goods has become much more sophisticated and has
exploded into an enormous business that costs the world economy hundreds of billions of dollars every year. It used to be that a
savvy buyer could quickly spot a fake. I remember being im-
pressed as a kid by Rolex watches, back in the late seventies. I was
aware that you could buy a fake Rolex, but I knew it was a piece of
junk. Because my father is a jeweler, I might have been more aware
of the counterfeit issue than most kids, since it was something I
would occasionally discuss with my dad. He imported precious
stones and pearls, and used to travel regularly on business to
Japan, Hong Kong, Bangkok, and other parts of Asia. That was almost forty years ago, but even then he would pass countless street
vendors offering a wide range of counterfeited products. As an
amusement, on a given trip he might bring back a Louis Vuitton
wallet, a Cartier watch, or a pair of Gucci sunglasses—all fakes.
But back then, if you compared a real one with a fake one side by
side, you could tell right away which was which by the quality of
material and the workmanship. Now there are counterfeiters that
invest significant amounts of money in producing a near-real version of the product they are looking to knock off. Occasionally,
only an expert can tell the difference.

   Counterfeiters have become very skilled, aided by advances in technology and encouraged by greater economic incentives as luxury goods fetch ever higher prices. Fakes used to be cheap junk, but now their apparent quality often rivals that of the original. With the best color printers and a few supplies, counterfeiters can reproduce all sorts of tickets—everything from sold-out shows to the big game to the local college game—and make them all look real. The combination of cheap labor and improved technology means that there are ever more powerful ways to make duplications today. As auction culture gets bigger and bigger, the incentive to counterfeit will grow, and the sophistication of knockoffs will grow, too. The potential payoff is so great that counterfeiters actually produce fake Rolex watches in 18-carat gold!

Counterfeit products can truly damage a company's brand and business. As fake products enter the market, several things begin to happen. First—and this is especially true for luxury goods—the brand erodes as consumers perceive it to be less exclusive as they see it flood the market. Counterfeits are not really made of the same quality and can disappoint consumers who think they are buying the real thing—when a counterfeit wallet begins to fall apart, the faithful but tricked customer blames the brand. The famous cream-colored Burberry plaid with its taupe lines and thin red striping is one of the most frequently faked trademarks, and that fact has had devastating consequences for the brand's image. Burberry has since become an example of what can happen when counterfeiters get the upper hand. After an earthshaking tsunami hit southeast Asia at the end of 2004, the Blackpool *Gazette* in the United Kingdom reported that the Lancashire County Council had decided to send confiscated counterfeit clothing to aid the victims rather than dumping it in a landfill. Lancashire officials agreed that it was a good idea to donate the clothes, which included fake Burberrys, but one official did point out that counterfeiting profits gangs. (One of the men responsible for the Madrid train bombings in 2004 dealt in fake designer goods, according to the Anti-Counterfeiting Group, an international organization.) Burberry's reputation suffered even more when pubs in the UK began prohibiting anyone wearing the famous plaid cap from entering. "Burberry is no longer a symbol of luxury, taste and refinement, but has become a uniform for loutish, drunken hooligans, known today as chavs—men and women more likely to pick a fight than be picked for the world's best-dressed list," the *Financial Times* reported. The company quickly scrapped the notorious caps.

The traditional response to counterfeiting threats has been to take aggressive action. Typically, a company will hire investigators to pursue counterfeiters and work closely with law enforcement to take action. Many companies also incorporate anticounterfeiting measures into product development by designing products that are difficult to copy. No matter what they do, however, the counterfeiters will always find a way to copy it. Rolex puts a serial number on its watches, but the fakes have serial numbers, too.

Predictably, counterfeits are also big sellers in the online marketplace, and there's a sordid history of sellers trying to pass off fakes as the real thing. Shortly after eBay took off, eBay halls of shame sprung up on Web sites dedicated to teaching shoppers how to see the difference between a Chinatown special and the real thing. In a sign of how widespread the problem is, the Federal Trade Commission found that in 2004, Internet auction fraud accounted for the top category of consumer fraud complaints. The FTC also reported that the number of complaints filed for the Internet auction category jumped from 51,003 in 2002 to 98,653 in 2004. The sale of these copycats clearly presents a pressing challenge to brand managers and retailers, and the explosion in online sales of fakes quickly became a particular concern. But it's important to remember that vast quantities of counterfeits are sold through channels other than eBay and other online sites. Street vendors that sell knockoffs are so popular in New York that there are bus trips that bring shoppers to the city just to shop the streets. Counterfeits are even being sold by mainstream retailers. In a prominent case in 2000, the retail chain Daffy's bought hundreds of Gucci bags from what was thought to be a reputable supplier. A Daffy's representative took one of the bags to a Gucci store to have it authenticated and the clerk called it genuine, comparing it to other bags in the store, but the bags turned out to be exceptionally well made fakes.

The auction culture hasn't created the counterfeit problem— not by a long shot—though the online market certainly poses special challenges. With the coming of auction culture, executives across the globe will be confronting challenges as relevant and potentially lethal as the challenges executives faced with the arrival of the automobile at the turn of the last century. Many companies have taken a shortsighted approach to contending with booming sales of knockoffs on eBay and other sites, attempting to shut down trading of their goods online altogether. But in doing so, they risk throwing out the baby with the bathwater. The fact is that the development of robust secondary online sales for their goods presents companies with many exciting opportunities to strengthen brand loyalty and grow their sales, but the initial reaction of too many companies has been to simply try to clamp down. That strategy is not only ineffective, it's actually high risk.

If some companies had their way, there would be no eBay or Amazon or Yahoo! or any other company that hosted an exchange where their goods could be traded. If you ask them, auction culture is their nightmare. But fighting auction culture is like trying to shut down the Internet. There is no stopping it. Business leaders don't have to adore auction culture, but if they want to succeed, they'll acknowledge its existence and address it in their plans for the future. There are ways to combat the sale of fakes, and companies should embrace these methods rather than attack the auction market generally. EBay has even taken initiatives in facilitating the policing of auctions of fakes. Companies should make use of the tools provided, rather than combating the auction services, which, as we'll see, hasn't worked anyway.

The role models should be the more visionary companies that are discovering the incredible potential of auction culture and how they can benefit from harnessing it. Unafraid of the competition, these companies have greeted the online exchange platforms with open arms. And like the first retailers that made it possible to shop through their Web sites, these companies have watched their creative approaches pay off.

I'LL SEE YOU IN COURT

It was only a matter of time before someone dragged eBay into court in a move to attempt to chill the sale of their goods in the secondary market. The motive was to control the flow of product, but the legal issue that had to be decided by the courts was the level of eBay's responsibility for the wares hawked on its pages.

Oddly, the pivotal court case against eBay didn't come from a towering luxury brand. Instead, it centered on *Manson,* a documentary about convicted murderer and cult leader Charles Manson. When filmmaker Robert Hendrickson noticed pirated copies of his 1972 documentary on eBay in December 2000, he sent the company a cease-and-desist letter. He asked eBay to pull the items because of copyright infringement or face a court battle. EBay responded by suggesting that Hendrickson enroll in its Verified Rights Owner program, known as VeRO, to pull the auctions himself.

Introduced in 1998, VeRO is now a large part of eBay's antifraud efforts. VeRO came about as the result of both legal and public relations concerns that had pushed the growing company towards investing more and more resources and personnel into cracking down on trading in fakes. In 1997, eBay hired corporate lawyer Brad Handler, who came up with VeRO's precursor, the Legal Buddy program. Companies and celebrities searched the site for fakes and then "buddied" with eBay employees to report them. Beginning the next year with VeRO, companies could join as members and could then target eBay auctions that infringe on their copyrighted or trademarked items. Here's how VeRO works: member companies are responsible for trolling eBay for knockoffs. When they find listings for counterfeits, they report the listings to eBay, which then pulls the auctions on behalf of the companies. EBay describes VeRO on its Web site as a program that "works to ensure that items listed for auction do not infringe upon the copyright, trademark or other intellectual property rights of third parties. VeRO Program participants may identify and request removal of allegedly infringing auction listings."

Instead of enrolling in VeRO, however, Hendrickson sued eBay and two sellers, charging that eBay itself was liable for selling unauthorized copies of his documentary. The case turned out to be the test for the federal Digital Millennium Copyright Act of 1998, a version of basic copyright law that applies to the Internet. In 2001, federal judge Robert J. Kelleher pointed out that eBay is not just some small site for electronic classified ads. "EBay's own website describes itself as 'the world's largest online marketplace,'" he wrote. He also acknowledged that the copies of Hendrickson's documentary sold on eBay were clearly pirated. But despite these observations, Kelleher ruled that "eBay is not actively involved in the listing, bidding, sale and delivery of any item offered for sale on its website." In other words, eBay isn't actually involved in each exchange, it just provides a platform for trade. Kelleher noted that eBay had proven it was never actually in possession of the illegal copies, and so he concluded that "the record shows that eBay does not have the right and ability to control the infringing activity at issue."

The Hendrickson case defined eBay's legal status and absolved the company from liability when sellers and buyers engage in illegal behavior. Everything seemed settled in eBay's favor. But Hendrickson was a documentary filmmaker who had made only one film, according to the entry in the comprehensive Internet Movie Database. Enormous companies with millions on the line decided to launch their own legal battles, testing the extent of eBay's worldwide responsibility.

The first large company to go after eBay for counterfeit sales was Rolex, even before Judge Kelleher had handed down his decision on the Manson documentary case. As my friend Howard had observed, fake Rolexes really are everywhere. When he rolled down his window, eBay wasn't involved. So eBay clearly isn't the root problem, but Rolex sued nonetheless. In April 2001, Montres Rolex SA and Rolex affiliates sued eBay's European subsidiaries in Germany. Rolex clearly viewed the online auction platform as a threat. Instead of embracing it and finding ways to incorporate the new phenomenon into its business, Rolex charged the German eBay site with unfair competition as well as with violating Rolex's trademarks. Rolex sought damages and asked that eBay stop listing its watches online. EBay's legal defense was that eBay is a listing service, not a store. All eBay does is offer a platform for sales, rather than participating in the sales themselves. Furthermore, since third parties put items up for sale, create the descriptions, upload photographs for listings, and establish opening bids, third-party sellers are the ones responsible for selling counterfeits, not eBay. Besides, eBay argued, Rolex had the power to police the sales of fakes because it had enrolled in the VeRO program.

The VeRO program was not without its detractors, but it demonstrated that eBay was aware of the problem and working to develop a specific strategy to deal with it, and that initiative gave a strong boost to the company's legal defense. Heading into the Rolex lawsuit in Germany, eBay sounded a confident note, filing a statement with the United States Securities and Exchange Commission that the company "believes that it has meritorious defenses against this claim and intends to defend itself vigorously." Since Rolex had become an active VeRO member, benefiting from the program's mechanisms, it was implicitly endorsing the VeRO program and the assumptions behind it. The German counterpart to eBay had developed its own similar program, Verifiziert Rechte Inhaber, which was known by the German acronym VeRI. Rolex had decided not to enroll in that particular program. As a result, a German court ruled in eBay's favor in December 2002. Rolex decided to appeal, taking its case before the higher regional court of Düsseldorf. The appeal was decided in eBay's favor in February 2004. That didn't spell the end of Rolex's efforts, though. The company won a case that year, in March, against another European online exchange, Ricardo.de AG, before the German federal supreme court, based on a related argument. But as of summer 2005, Rolex had not taken any action to try to bring an appeal of its case against eBay before the German federal supreme court.

While the Rolex tussle continued overseas, the auction platform faced more attacks back in the United States. Tiffany and Company filed suit against eBay in New York district court in June 2004, claiming that eBay encouraged the sale of tens of thousands of pieces of fake Tiffany jewelry and, in the process, devalued the 150-year-old Tiffany brand. The company said that its own research showed that 73 percent of the listings on eBay that identified goods as Tiffany jewelry were clearly fakes, and that only 5 percent were clearly genuine. They wanted detailed financial information on how much eBay had profited from allowing the exchange of fakes through its sites. Tiffany sought damages of $1 million for each type of fake Tiffany merchandise sold on eBay.

"The consumer gets deceived, Tiffany gets damaged and eBay gets its fees," Tiffany lawyer James Swire of Dorsey & Whitney told the New York *Daily News.* Attorney Patti Waldmeir, U.S. legal columnist for the *Financial Times,* explained the basis of the lawsuit in a June 28, 2004, article, "Let the Online Buyer Be-ware." "EBay says it is perfectly happy to close down every fake Tiffany auction that it knows about and that it already does some limited monitoring of its own," Waldmeir wrote. "But it cannot shoulder the whole burden of keeping fakes off its site: rights owners like Tiffany have got to help out." Tiffany, she went on, says it takes too much time to monitor listings. It wanted eBay to automatically shut down listings on discounted Tiffany items.

An October 3, 2003, "E-Commerce Report" in the *New York Times* business section offered a glimpse of the way the allegedly fake Tiffany jewelry changed hands through an online exchange. The previous month, the *Times* reported, a posting went up on a discussion board at FatWallet.com announcing that a Tiffany heart-pendant necklace was selling for only $47 at Overstock.com—a bar-gain. Grateful posts arrived at the message board from various buyers, but so too did ominous-sounding messages. "Customers complained on FatWallet and to Overstock that the silver lacked luster or was gouged, and that the 'Tiffany & Co.' lettering was illegible," the *Times* reported. "And they complained that the jewelry arrived in boxes of a different hue from Tiffany's famous robin's-egg blue."

Overstock suspended sales on the item after 1,200 had been sold and began offering refunds to disgruntled customers. Its own investigation determined that the items in question had been purchased from a Canadian distributor who had bought them from the Italian division of Tiffany. To back up this claim, it posted a copy of the invoice for that sale. But Mark L. Aaron, a Tiffany spokesman, told the *Times,* "The thing was a fake." That should have been obvious, he said, since the difference in price was enough to prove that the items were not genuine. Tiffany, he said, "does not sell overstocked items, and our vendors aren't allowed to either. You only buy authentic Tiffany product at our stores and boutiques and on our Web site and catalog." Convincing the public of that message could be difficult, though, given the brisk trade in "Tiffany" items that continues at eBay and other online exchanges. More than $1.5 million per month worth of Tiffany products is traded on eBay alone. Tiffany couldn't easily control what customers did with their products. After all, customers didn't sign a binding contract at Tiffany and Company declaring that they would never resell any of their purchases.

Few legal analysts give Tiffany much of a chance of winning its suit against eBay. *The Economist* summed it up well in an editorial in its July 3, 2004, issue: "EBay should not be held responsible for verifying the authenticity of Tiffany's, or any other company's, products," the article said. "It would be like ordering newspapers to take responsibility for the authenticity of the goods and services which are offered for sale in their classified advertising. In the end, it is the job of a brand's owner to defend its intellectual property rights, although that owner clearly deserves the active co-operation of any middleman whose services are being used to peddle fakes." Success will be built on trust, the article continued, but until that happens, let the buyer beware. Subsequently, Tiffany and Company has used the VeRO program to shut down nearly nineteen thousand eBay auctions.

STRONG-ARMING SELLERS

Companies besides Tiffany have employed VeRO aggressively, but not always discriminately. Some have used it as a way to discourage sellers from trading certain products altogether in the secondary marketplace. Right from the start of VeRO, eBay received complaints from sellers who believed that some companies were indiscriminately shutting down auctions, purposefully closing legitimate auctions involving secondhand items. The motive, the sellers argued, was to keep retail profits higher. Several sources document how a well-meaning charity tried to sell Mary Kay cosmetics that had been donated to it. They found themselves being hounded by lawyers.

Texan Mary Kay Ash founded her cosmetics business in 1963, based on the concept of giving women a chance to earn extra money as independent consultants who bought the cosmetics wholesale and sold them at retail prices. Mary Kay products became purse staples. Yet the very same company that has empowered and fostered the independence of more than 1.3 million consultants worldwide also has a policy against allowing those same consultants to sell Mary Kay products on eBay. While Mary Kay consultants are awarded jeweled pins for accomplishing high sales levels, the no-eBay policy effectively puts a potentially lucrative path beyond reach. Mary Kay is a VeRO member and its description on eBay shouts in a large, bold red font, "Buy Only Authentic Mary Kay® Products from Authorized Mary Kay® Independent Beauty Consultants." The Mary Kay independent contractors argue that they are just auctioning off overstocked moisturizer and eye cream that wouldn't sell otherwise. In 2003, a Mary Kay legal representative told AuctionBytes, an online exchange news site, that buyers could be purchasing opened or used products from eBay; there's no guarantee. But Mary Kay's eBay policy doesn't appear to be working, despite its

VeRO membership. A recent search for "Mary Kay" on eBay pulled up thousands of listings containing plenty of product. In fact, more than $25,000 a day is traded in Mary Kay products on eBay.

I've seen firsthand how the strategy of subverting the secondary market can backfire. Several months ago, I watched a woman try to sell a Chanel skirt through an eBay dropshop. It's not surprising that she would consider trying to get some money for it. After all, shoppers were definitely looking for Chanel on eBay. Why wouldn't they? It was the brand that Coco Chanel, the originator of the "little black dress," had built. The iconic label had taken women out of corsets and put them in soft jersey, all while maintaining cutting-edge style. After designer Karl Lagerfeld revitalized the pedigreed fashion house in the 1980s, Chanel became synonymous with chic.

The woman who wanted to sell her Chanel at the dropshop had a skirt that no longer fit. She was planning to put the proceeds from the auction towards a new Chanel outfit, but the auction consultant quickly looked at the label and politely informed the customer that her skirt could not be accepted for auction. Why? Because Chanel was notorious for causing trouble in the secondary market.

The company's leadership thinks that the secondary market is enabling piracy, hurting the primary market, and devaluing their brand. Chanel didn't file suit against eBay; others had proven that this wasn't an effective way to control the secondary market. Instead, Chanel began using eBay's own tool for combating counterfeits and copyright infringements, VeRO, to choke auctions of Chanel products—fake or, in many cases, the real thing. All to discourage facilitators from taking in their products to begin with. EBay's management has confirmed that this type of behavior is widely used by several prominent brands to discourage trading in their goods.

"Beware Designer Items!" AuctionBytes editor Ina Steiner admonished her readers back in 2001. Her case in point turned out to be Chanel. Like the aforementioned dropshop, Steiner's readers informed her that Chanel had been shutting down legitimate auctions on eBay. Steiner reported that a reader wrote to her wondering why eBay had pulled her auction of a Chanel necklace that she had originally bought at an estate sale. Steiner wrote to Chanel on behalf of her confounded reader and was told that Chanel believed that the necklace was a fake and that the seller could, of course, go try to get it authenticated and then auction it again.

Chanel's decision makers no doubt believe they are protecting the company's interests by shutting down auctions and trying to dissuade anyone from reselling their products. But I would argue that they have not thought their approach through to its logical conclusion. While companies like Chanel might be able to dissuade trade in their goods and benefit from it in the short run, this move may well come back to haunt them in the future.

If Chanel could effectively prevent consumers from selling their merchandise through eBay and similar sites, ultimately there wouldn't be a secondary market for those goods. Without any secondary market for Chanel or even with just a weak and isolated one, many consumers who would have bought Chanel products will opt for some other brand. The Chanel customer I saw thwarted in the effort to sell her skirt walked away from the experience feeling that Chanel had picked her pocket by denying her the skirt's resale value. If Chanel continues this policy, soon the world will be full of people like this woman who have soured on the Chanel brand despite many years of loyalty. If Chanel's products develop a low value in the secondary market in the long run because of this policy, its brand value will deteriorate accordingly. I wonder whether Chanel executives have considered this outcome.

Other businesses have taken innovative, forward-thinking approaches to the challenges, and opportunities, presented by the growth of auction culture, and their initial risks have paid off.

RISKY BUSINESS

Imagine if, instead of suing eBay, Tiffany had created its own exchange in order to compete head-on with eBay's marketplace.

Amazon is a company that saw the world changing and decided to make a bold move to own certain channels of the secondary market before it was too late. After a series of trials and errors, Amazon's aggression worked out to be a brilliant strategy.

In March 1999, Amazon decided to get into the auction business, hoping to shake up eBay by sweeping up LiveBid.com. The new online auction site Amazon started guaranteed purchases of up to $250 and offered $10 Amazon gift certificates to auction participants for a limited time. The online retailer also preregistered its eight million existing customers to its auction platform, creating a widespread and ready set of participants. That way, Amazon customers could just log in to the site as they always had and start participating in auctions instead of having to fill out online forms from scratch. Amazon CEO Jeff Bezos put one of the company's original desks, made from a door, on the block for the charity auction that marked the auction site's start.

Later that year, Amazon partnered with Sotheby's to boost its reputation. Sotheby's experts authenticated auction items, which should have given the site an extra edge. Instead, it failed. The two companies cited confusion over which site was for which kind of auction. Furthermore, customers were irritated at having to register all of their contact and credit card information twice. Even after combining the two sites into Sothebys.Amazon.com, however, confusion lingered and the venture never managed to become profitable. The two giants announced in 2000 that they were closing their site. Sotheby's went on to attempt a partnership with eBay. That, too, failed to turn a profit. In 2003, Sotheby's announced that it was closing its entire online auction site but would continue to use eBay's platform for select live auctions. Some observers remarked that Sotheby's high-end auctions had seemed out of place in the casual online format. Others pointed to a Justice Department investigation into commission-fixing at the auction house, which threw the company's credibility into doubt at the time. President Diana D. Brooks ultimately pleaded guilty. The real reason may actually have just been that despite their apparent similarities, they are completely different businesses that operate under different fundamentals: traditional auctioneers are concerned with the seller and not the buyer, which is the opposite of the online model, which relies on high levels of customer service and merchandising because there is no tangible interaction.

Even though high-end auction houses had backed away from the live online exchange platform, Amazon hung tough and its auction division began to thrive. (Meanwhile, typing "sothebys.amazon.com" into an Internet browser will still redirect Web surfers to Amazon's current auction site.)

By 2000, eBay and Amazon were on a course of competitive one-upmanship. In June of that year, eBay announced that it was buying Half.com for more than $312 million. CEO Meg Whitman had decided she liked the book exchange giant so much after buying a fly-fishing guide there that she arranged the deal. By the end of the year, Amazon had taken a radical step to transform its business. It built an exchange and incorporated it prominently within its marketplace that November. Soon, the exchange allowed users to post listings for used books, compact disks, and other items alongside the identical listing Amazon had for new goods in its core retail business. On the surface, the move seemed crazy. It was like Tiffany allowing its customers to open up a prominent stand to sell used Tiffany jewelry right next to the entrance of its flagship store on Fifth Avenue. Amazon seemed to be cannibalizing its core business. But the situation wasn't that dissimilar from a car dealer selling a used car right next to the new version of the same model. This was Amazon's forward-thinking response to a powerful shift in the marketplace, and ultimately it helped the company stay competitive against eBay.

Amazon's move paid off. Third-party sellers, which are outside merchants from individuals to large companies that sell their products through Amazon's marketplace and exchange have also become an important source of revenue. The *Los Angeles Times* reported in 2005 that Amazon's 900,000 third-party sellers made up about a quarter of the company's overall sales.

INTERN AUTHENTICATORS

Another leading company, Kate Spade, has devised an innovative approach to the problem of the auctioning of counterfeits.

Barbara Kolsun is Kate Spade's senior vice president and ruthless general counsel. She has such a vehement distaste for counterfeits and counterfeiters that she once made a friend smash a counterfeit Rolex with a hammer in her kitchen, according to a profile of Kolsun in the *New York Times*. "This is something you have to feel really strongly and passionately about," she told me. Kolsun's grandfather and father worked in factories and other family members were in the production business. Kolsun was in Vietnam teaching intellectual property law when she heard a story that reinforced her dedication to fighting copyright infringement. She said, "One man stood up and said, 'My wife is one of the most famous singers in Vietnam, and the day after her first CD was released, it was completely pirated.' So why should she stay in Vietnam? She can't make a living as a singer. She's not going to get any royalties. . . . What's the incentive for anybody to be creative if people so cavalierly knock things off?"

When the *Boston Globe* collected advice on spotting fakes, Kolsun advised that shoppers buy the Kate Spade label directly from authorized retailers and avoid getting it through online auctions or flea markets. Don't get her wrong—in an article for *Corporate Legal Times,* she told legal journalist Cathleen Flahardy that she hoped Tiffany would win its lawsuit against eBay, taking the policing burden off companies that included Kate Spade. Kolsun told me that while she is not an eBay fan, she has long recognized how large it is. From the time she arrived at Kate Spade in 2002, she knew that something had to be done to combat the counterfeiters. "I knew there was probably a big eBay problem," she told me. "I didn't know how big it was, and when I saw how big it was, I picked up the phone and called my law school and said I needed interns."

Kolsun hired a team of law students from her alma mater, Benjamin N. Cardozo School of Law in New York. Now a team of ten interns spends twenty hours a week combing online auctions, mainly eBay, looking for fakes. She says that Kate Spade has a detailed archive of its collections so it's been straightforward for the interns to spot counterfeits from uploaded photos on listings. Sometimes it's as simple as spotting a print that has never appeared on a real Kate Spade bag. Other times it can be as subtle as a fabric label with letters that are slightly off. "Everybody has occasionally—rarely, but occasionally—misidentified," Kolsun says. "We just reinstate the auction. We've never been sued, or threatened to sue. Almost all the time we're right because we know our products so well." The work is constant, but the effort appears to be working. Kate Spade continues to be a prominent luxury brand, growing at a healthy pace.

EMBRACING EXCHANGE

A number of other companies, from the United States Postal Service (USPS) to Dell Inc., have focused on the opportunities presented by the growth of auction culture.

The USPS jumped into Internet retailing early, launching its online store in 1999 amid worries that e-mail would edge out snail mail. Since then, the independent government agency has kept its eye on ways to use the Internet to its advantage. All sorts of shipping services regularly vie for customers on eBay—the largest dropshops have partnerships with UPS and the United States Postal Service. Even though competition has remained fierce for shipping supplies and services, USPS continues to leap forward. In February 2004, eBay and USPS partnered to come up with a shipping cost calculator that assists users in figuring out their final costs. Then, later that year, the two partnered again to offer free USPS Priority Mail shipping boxes with the eBay logo on them. Customers can pay for USPS labels and print them through eBay. The *Orange County Register* reported in 2005 that post offices around the country had started offering free seminars on how to use the Internet auction site. One Anaheim business owner told the paper that the unexpected seminars had changed her thinking about the United States Postal Service and she was considering using them to ship her sales.

Dell Inc., the largest manufacturer and seller of computers in the world, has also taken a proactive approach to turning the secondary market into a plus. Dell sells direct to consumers—that was the company's bold stroke of genius—and it has brilliantly perceived the secondary market as another robust channel for reaching the consumer.

In the late 1990s, Dell joined an alliance called the Fair-Market auction network with other heavy hitters like Microsoft and Lycos in the hope of competing with eBay. By 2001, though, FairMarket had lost millions on the venture and finally decided to make a deal with eBay to run listings on its site. But Dell didn't let that experience discourage it from participating in the auction culture altogether. It put together an entire division dedicated to selling discontinued computers and accessories at auction on eBay. Like any company, Dell faces the issue of what to do with inventory that grows obsolete. They want to get rid of it in a timely manner and they understand that they can use the secondary market as a legitimate sales channel. Dell also understands that beyond moving their inventories more productively, maintaining an active presence on eBay and other similar sites has the benefit of ensuring that more customers will get to know their brand, boosting the resale value of their products. Since 2001, Dell has featured a special shop on eBay called Dell Financial Services just for selling off-lease refurbished computer products, computers that have been returned at the conclusion of a lease, usually by large corporations.

Sears, one of the world's largest retailers, has also adopted eBay as a venue to liquidate items that have been returned to their stores by customers. Many of the products sold on the site are clearly represented with a qualifying "Note: this is an open-box, used item." Sears opened its liquidation center on eBay in June 2003 and sold off forty thousand items in the most recent twelve-month period.

Other companies have made clever use of the power of auction culture as a form of production or brand promotion. In a 2003 article, *Forbes* magazine highlighted Nissan in a group of companies that were building buzz for their brands by using eBay in creative ways. So how did they do it? Jeffrey Kowalczyk of TBWA/Chiat/Day, which handled the Nissan account, had this to say about Nissan's reintroducing its 350Z sports car, originally produced in 1996. "Our research told us that the same guys who were Z enthusiasts in the '70s and '80s are on eBay Motors today," he said. As the article went on to explain, Kowalczyk came up with the idea to "auction the first revamped 350Z off the assembly line on eBay, with the proceeds going to charity." The car ultimately went for $95,000, far more than its sticker price. Not to mention all the free publicity that Nissan received just for launching a new car!

Like Nissan, Disney has seized on eBay as a way to promote

its name and move merchandise that otherwise would lie dormant in a warehouse. In 2000, the Walt Disney Internet Group first started linking to eBay auctions from its site. Disney executives opened their "vault" and poured thousands of items onto the auction block. When Mickey Mouse turned seventy-five in 2005, Disney partnered with Sotheby's to run a celebrity auction of seventy-five unique statues of the grinning icon. It accepted online and absentee bids through eBay, and the proceeds will go to a number of charities.

Forbes reported in 2003 that IBM marked the ThinkPad's tenth anniversary by auctioning off laptops that had been autographed by Sylvester Stallone and Walter Cronkite. Scores of other large retail companies have followed suit, deciding to participate in the online auction phenomenon by building storefront sites on eBay. Some of the big names now include Sears, Hewlett Packard, and KitchenAid. Consumer electronics giant Toshiba also harnessed auction culture by creating a trade-in program to recoup used products in exchange for money. Toshiba can then turn around and auction the same items on eBay through its own eBay store to turn a profit.

We are still at the very early stages of auction culture, and the landscape of strategies and responses is just beginning to be charted. Trying to thwart the auction market makes no sense, and ignoring the challenges and opportunities will only risk significant losses of customers, revenues, and brand value in the future. The change is under way, and the forces are great—but businesses need a sound roster of strategies for embracing auction culture. In the next chapter we'll explore a number of vital steps that companies can take in order to contend with the challenges and harness the potential.

8 SETTING A COURSE
Winning Business Strategies

I t's an old story, and always the same: the sooner decision makers are equipped with reliable information about how a marketplace will shift, the stronger their competitive advantage will be. Smart businesspeople are always on the lookout for insight into how they can best adapt to or, better yet, take advantage of a changing world. What if you were a buggy whip manufacturer who happened to be in Detroit, Michigan, on September 27, 1908, the day the Model T rolled out of Henry Ford's Piquette Plant? At the time, no one understood that this automobile would become a harbinger of the future. Would you have recognized the implications of the event? Say that someone gave you, the buggy whip maker, a heads-up and said, "You see that automobile? It will replace the need for buggies. Not only will everybody want one, they'll be affordable, too." What would you have done?

Buggy whips, of course, went the way of the slide rule, the 8-track, and Sony's Betamax video format. One buggy whip maker who got out ahead of the curve was Henry A. Strong, who cofounded another company that's had to cope with its own fair share of innovation. In 1881, Strong invested in a new endeavor with family friend George Eastman, based in their native Rochester, New York—the photographic film company later called Eastman Kodak. At its zenith in the 1970s, Kodak sold more cameras than all of its competitors combined, but the digital camera explosion forced the company to change drastically to stay afloat. Throughout the late 1990s, Kodak began diversifying its business, collaborating with companies such as Intel and Adobe Systems. Then it scaled back, cutting thousands of jobs and closing its single-use camera factory in the United States. In a bold move that startled many photographers, Kodak announced plans in 2005 to stop making black-and-white photographic paper, the kind that professional photographers use for printing out images. By slicing away some areas of its operations, Kodak has been redeploying its capital to expand in other directions, notably purchasing a company that makes image-sensor chips for cell phones.

Ignoring the new rules of engagement can be disastrous, as *Encyclopaedia Britannica*'s recent tumble demonstrates. The encyclopedia was founded in 1768 by three Scottish printers and later sold to a succession of American owners who ultimately turned it into a hugely successful business that peaked at more than $650 million in sales in 1990. Shortly thereafter, the market for printed encyclopedias suddenly disappeared, forcing the owners to sell the business for a fraction of its book value.

Encyclopaedia Britannica simply failed to grasp how fundamentally computers had changed the terms of the reference business. In their book, *Blown to Bits: How the New Economics of Information Transforms Strategy,* Philip Evans and Thomas Wurster argue that parents purchased encyclopedias in order to feel as though they were doing enough to ensure that their children would do well in school. As computer prices approached the cost of encyclopedias, parents opted instead to assuage their guilt by buying PCs bundled with Encarta, an encyclopedia CD-ROM. "But with the mindset of the executives of the [Britannica] business, steeped in a culture of scholarly values and self-confident from a history of unbroken success, it is extraordinarily hard to understand early enough that conventional industry definitions are obsolete," the authors write. And it was their legacy mind-set operating in the face of cultural change that caused the company to crash.

Evan's observations are as relevant now as they were then. With the coming of auction culture, executives across the globe will be confronting challenges as transformative—and potentially lethal—as the challenges executives faced at the arrival of the automobile at the turn of the last century and the Internet in the mid-1990s. In the same stroke, auction culture will create a universe of new business opportunities.

Fortunately, there is still time for businesses, both big and small, to formulate effective plans for coping with the challenges and taking advantage of the opportunities. Here is an essential list of options to consider.

Adopt Authentication Services
and Embedded Technologies

Since so many companies have been legitimately concerned about the rampant production and sale of fake versions of their products in the auction marketplace, let's start by addressing that issue. Instead of killing the messenger—or rather, as the case has tended to be, suing the messenger—why not thwart would-be counterfeiters before they can even consider gluing on a fake label? Sadly, many companies out there today, including some very prominent brands, cannot authenticate their merchandise, and without authentication capabilities, they have no control over the secondary market. Some companies are in such bad shape when it comes to authenticity that employees are left looking at old catalogs and guessing whether a product in question was made by the company or not. Recall the case of the Gucci knockoffs that were sold to Daffy's? Even Gucci's own store clerk couldn't spot that the bags were fakes. In that case, Gucci sued Daffy's over trademark infringement, but Daffy's ultimately won the lawsuit, in part because it had acted in good faith, according to the court decision. After all, a Gucci employee had initially validated the item as real.

New technology is simplifying the authentication process by making it easier to identify fakes. That said, forward-looking companies will need to develop their own authentication standards and then educate their employees accordingly. The next step is to put new technology to work. Not only will it foil counterfeiters, but it will assure customers that the real thing does exist.

Some companies track a photo of the product against a serial number. Cartier can etch a store's signature and a serial number onto the girdle of its diamonds. DuPont makes three-dimensional holograms as well as covert forensic product identification. Car manufacturers use VIN numbers registered with the government.

One powerful technology that is being used for authentication is the microchip. There are already a number of companies that manufacture microchips for authenticity purposes, including A-Tag Authentication, a company that was started by two police officers in Australia to capture a growing niche. They produce microchips that can be embedded in sports memorabilia to ensure that they're genuine. Each authentic piece of memorabilia gets a microchip with a unique fifteen-digit code on it that corresponds to a database entry containing a description of the item. The microchip is then coated with a tamper-proof label; a hand-held scanner reveals the code underneath. Major sports associations in Australia embraced the technology after fakes flooded the memorabilia market. Only signatures that have been witnessed by designated officials and sports managers qualify for the chip. When a series of three autographed lithographs, issued to commemorate a match between Andre Agassi and Roger Federer at the billion-dollar Burj Al Arab Hotel in Dubai, were sold to raise money for UNICEF in 2005, the pieces were protected with A-Tag Authentication.

The advent of a form of microchip called "radio frequency identification tags" (RFID) has had a transformative effect on a variety of businesses, from pharmaceuticals to automobiles. These tiny devices can be either active or passive, but when a certain radio signal hits them, they send out a response. Although they aren't without their controversial side, several companies are making inroads on testing. In 2005, RFID tags came in several frequencies, contained identification information that could be picked up and read with special scanners, and could be made thinner than a piece of paper. Starting in January 2005, retail giant Wal-Mart asked its largest suppliers to use the tags on the pallets they delivered to distribution centers. One supplier, Hampton International Products, went a step further and used RFID technology to streamline its business. Hampton, based in California, manufactures locks, hardware, and security products. Rick Tysdal, Hampton Products' COO, told *Wireless News* in 2005 that the company is working on tracking every single product it manufactures using the technology. That's potentially a very wise move for a company that sells locks and security lights. Other retailers are testing out ways to use RFID. All the merchandise in Prada's SoHo store in New York City is tagged, for example, and Michelin is working on tagging its tires.

Companies that care about their brands must be able to identify every product they are currently producing and have a tracking system in place so that they will be able to recognize each one far into the future. While undertaking this procedure sounds obvious, I know of several companies (which will remain anonymous) that have been producing luxury goods for decades and don't do this. Their employees can't tell if one of their products from ten years ago is actually the real thing. If these companies don't start implementing systems to authenticate their products, their brands will remain vulnerable and they risk losing value in the future. If they can't identify their product today, how will anyone be able to authenticate it tomorrow or twenty years from now? Authenticity is a crucial enforcer of brand value. Now, more than ever, counterfeiting can hurt businesses that don't respond to these issues. Imagine an innocent (or a not so innocent) shopper buying something fake on eBay and taking it to a store where the clerk can't figure out how to authenticate it. Now picture that shopper unknowingly exchanging their fake for the real thing. A key component to a brand is the ability to distinguish it from all the other ones out there. It's more important than ever to stand out. Businesses that don't recognize this will discover that their brand is trading out of control.

Before long, many high-priced products will include some version of an authentication microchip that can be baked into watches or jewelry and sewn into clothing. With the chip in place, it will take two seconds to scan it and get all the information about the product's manufacture and history. If a piece of clothing has been altered at some point, that information could also be included. Eventually, counterfeiters will try to fake the microchips as well, but the trick will be to stay one step ahead of them and to eliminate incentives for counterfeiters by making it easier for customers to identify which products are real and which are not.

Make Managing the Secondary Market an Integral Part of Your Business Model

In recognizing the importance of a liquid secondary market as a legitimate channel, business leaders will want to respond by proactively addressing the way their business interacts with the secondary-market channel. They should put executive-level employees in place to effectively manage the channel.

Think back to the 1990s, when the Internet started to surge

ahead and transformed everything. Companies hoping to harness the new technology set up whole departments to develop and manage an Internet strategy. What should the Web site look like? Should we even have a Web site? Should we allow people to buy or just browse? What happens once our competition sees what we carry? Is this good for our business or bad? Should we jump in early or wait to see where others go right or wrong? These were the questions pondered in the business meetings of many corporations at the dawn of the Internet.

Waves from the secondary marketplaces cascade into the primary marketplace and then recede again. As you'll see, if the secondary market is suddenly awash in one particular product, that can provide useful information about the primary market for the same product. The head of secondary-market sales will manage the channel just like a marketing vice president might manage the retail channel. These individuals will focus on managing the brand, merchandising, pricing, loyalty programs, and, most important, evaluating and monitoring how these factors affect the primary market for their company's products.

Businesses that develop core competencies in managing the secondary market for their products will enjoy significant advantages as they stay ahead of the curve. Those that do so will keep counterfeiters at bay by guaranteeing authenticity, and will thus gain the trust and loyalty of their clientele, increase their profits, have a firm grasp on what their sales figures really mean, and be adept at understanding the competition. The first step is to accept that the secondary market is real, and then act by staffing to the need.

Develop a Certified Pre-Owned
Program for Your Brand

The old adage "If you can't beat 'em, join 'em" holds true when exploring ways to manage your brand in the secondary market. Rather than watch from the sidelines as other companies profit from the resale of their goods, brand producers should get in the game by developing a certified pre-owned category for their products. This has already been done in several markets, including the car market.

Starting in the early 1990s, the automobile industry made a move to snatch the secondary marketplace back from independent dealers. The popularity of leasing had flooded the marketplace with recently used cars that retained significant value. And soon they realized that unaffiliated dealers were making a healthy profit selling their previously owned cars in the secondary market. They wanted to participate in the profits derived from those transactions. In order to retain their customers, manufacturers such as Lexus, BMW, and Mercedes-Benz created new programs whereby customers could buy a used car that had been thoroughly inspected, certified as having been checked properly, and then put under a manufacturer's warranty. By developing a certified pre-owned program, they gained more control over their brand, using the secondary market to build and maintain relationships with customers and manage those relationships in the hopes that those same customers would buy a new car from them in the future.

This approach has paid off dramatically in the automobile business. The automotive research and marketing firm J.D. Power and Associates estimated in a 2005 study that nearly 38 percent of all late-model used-car sales at dealerships are certified pre-owned vehicles, up from 34 percent in the 2004 study's findings. Chrysler Group reported in 2005 that it had sold a record number of certified pre-owned vehicles in July, up 8 percent from the previous year. BMW, Porsche, and General Motors reported similar increases. The move to certify pre-owned vehicles shifted the marketplace, as well as consumers' assumptions about buying.

The same strategy works for other kinds of consumer brands. From luxury handbag designers to high-end baby stroller manufacturers like Bugaboo, companies can carve out this space in their market segment. They'll have a tremendous advantage over the typical online seller who can't offer the same guarantees as the company itself can.

There are several ways to play the certified pre-owned game. In order to establish this type of service, you can either form a partnership to outsource it or create a separate in-house division to manage the program. The advantage of managing the program from within is that you maintain control, but the disadvantage is that it may be viewed as a distraction to your core business. A partner company will need to acquire the goods (more on that later) and ultimately train employees or contractors to inspect and test products for quality so that the original manufacturer can issue a warranty and reattach its brand to the goods.

Golf club maker Callaway, famous for its Big Bertha driver, introduced a program called Trade In! Trade Up! in 2003 that offered customers the ability to trade in their old Callaway clubs for new ones through certain retailers. In 2004, Callaway solidified its trade-in program, buying out e-commerce partner FrogTrader, also known as Trade Up Commerce. Trade Up had primarily been responsible for liquidating used Callaway equipment. Callaway then licensed its brand name to Trade Up and trained Trade Up's employees to refurbish Callaway clubs according to the parent company's standards. "The used clubs are tested for flexibility, strength and performance, and then polished, painted, sand-blasted and given new grips," the *New York Times* reported in 2004, shortly after Callaway's program began. Callaway doesn't actually buy or sell the used products itself, but lets Trade Up Commerce assume the risk, Trade Up's chief marketing officer Brian Henley told the *Times*.

Trading in a used golf club creates value for golfers who would otherwise let their old clubs waste away in the closet. For example, a 2005 Big Bertha Fusion FT-3 driver trades for $240 and retails for about $500 new, although some online retailers offer it for close to $400. Trading it in would mean a couple hundred dollars in credit to put towards a new driver. The program has been extremely successful for Callaway. Callaway's director of global sales told the *Houston Chronicle* in 2004 that the program had already brought in thousands of trades. Giving millions of dollars' worth of discounts to customers guarantees significant goodwill, which translates to brand loyalty.

Callaway had intentionally created its certified pre-owned program for clubs based on similar programs taking hold in the automobile industry. Callaway vice president Larry Dorman told the *Tampa Tribune* in 2005 that the program, like those in the car industry, gave people who wouldn't usually be able to afford such a luxury a chance to be part of it. "When you have brand equity and people want to get your product, even if it has been driven a few miles, the value still holds," he said. The trade-in program fosters customer loyalty, which has translated into increasing revenue for the company.

Another example of a successful pre-owned program is one that my company, Portero, formed with Tourneau, the largest watch retailer in the world, to stabilize the experience for watch buyers in the secondary market. The secondary market for watches is rife with unscrupulous characters who pawn fake watches as real on eBay. Knowledge of this widespread behavior, coupled with the high value of luxury watches, has created a problem for both buyers, who hesitate to trust sellers they don't know, and legitimate sellers, who as a result lose both value and sales. Under the partnership, Tourneau trained the Portero staff on authentication techniques that meet their standards, and Portero uses those techniques to certify the authenticity of each watch it receives from customers. If a customer wants to sell a watch in the secondary market, Portero inspects it to make sure it is real and then issues a certificate, which uses Tourneau's brand as a seal of approval to authenticate and certify that the watch is real. The certification process can include research, testing, and even opening the watch to inspect the movement. On rare instances we go as far as sending the watch to the manufacturer to authenticate before issuing a certificate. Customers are selling through Portero, making the company a clearinghouse to eBay and other exchanges. Prospective buyers purchase the peace of mind that comes with knowing that the watch is authentic, and as a result they're willing to pay more. Tourneau not only extends its brand but also benefits directly by getting a percentage of each watch transaction on the Portero platform. Portero will be rolling out similar relationships in other categories as part of its business plan.

As an increasing number and variety of products come back into the marketplace through secondary channels, certified pre-owned programs can be a way to ensure that those products have been tested for safety and functionality as well as pedigree. As buyers are given the opportunity to rely on these programs, they'll demonstrate the willingness to pay for the knowledge that the $600 all-terrain stroller they just bought isn't defective and therefore safe for their child. As companies look for ways to protect their brands in the aftermarket, they will increasingly introduce similar certified pre-owned programs to maintain their products' integrities from one owner to the next.

Create Authorized Channels to the Secondary Market

If a company doesn't want to or can't sell directly to the public, it needs to designate a retailer to fulfill that role for it. Companies are advised to forge these partnerships early in the development of a brand, and then to work to establish them in customers' minds so that they recognize these places as legitimate sources for a particular product. This behavior is already widely practiced in the primary market, where luxury-goods manufacturers have designated partnerships with certain department stores in addition to their own stores. No retailers other than its authorized partners are allowed to sell its products officially.

Public awareness is a crucial element in this strategy. A brand's customers must know where to find products that are still backed by their parent companies as well as which shady places to avoid. If you go down Fifth Avenue in Manhattan to the thirties and forties, you will discover a wide variety of discount electronics stores. Few of them are authorized retailers, and knowledgeable consumers know to avoid them. Forget receiving a warranty. No returns, either. If it is defective, customers are generally left without recourse. The same thing can happen online, when buyers pay for products through unauthorized channels.

Establishing a partnership with an authorized resale channel partner allows you greater control over your brand in the secondary market and is largely analagous to establishing a retail channel partner. As businesses begin to understand how important the secondary marketplace is for their products, they will form these partnerships early (if they haven't already) and educate their customers as to which channels are legitimate and which ones aren't. Consider how well this has worked in the case of outlet malls.

Shoppers seeking authentic Prada go to a Prada store, where authenticity is guaranteed. Likewise, anyone who wants a brand-new iPod can go to an Apple store or find one at one of Apple's authorized retailers. These companies tend not to discount their items, but when a name like Burberry makes too many size 2 coats one season or J.Crew overstocks lime green plastic flip-flops, it makes sense to unload them somehow. But how to do it in a way that maintains the company's image? Enter Freeport, Kittery, Manchester. Outlet stores pull in bargain hunters like kids to a sprinkler in summer. They're a legitimate, familiar way to liquidate overstocked new items. Ralph Lauren was one of the first widely recognized brand names to officially use this strategy for selling slow-moving or slightly defective stock. In 1983, a Polo Ralph Lauren outlet moved in to Freeport, Maine, to take advantage of the customers flocking to L.L.Bean's expansive headquarters there. The *New York Times* called the location ideal for outlets— a town known for a store that was still far from major retailers. Others quickly followed Ralph Lauren's lead, turning Freeport into one of the top tourist destinations in the state. Outlet stores have become a major cash cow: in 2005, Ralph Lauren reported having 148 factory outlet stores compared to 127 regular stores.

Before the outlet stores, manufacturers, retailers tended to call up "jobbers" at the end of a season to bid on their goods in bulk. From there on out, the original brand owner generally had no control over how the merchandise was presented and sold. Outlet stores, easily distinguishable from flagship stores but carrying the same logo and service, became a recognized and profitable way to get rid of the leftovers while maintaining control over the selling process and preserving a brand's image.

Now the online versions of outlet malls, including Ashford.com and Bluefly.com, link far-removed but eager customers to well-known luxury fashion brands like Burberry, Gucci, and Fendi. Customers flock to these Internet outlets because they know they're getting the real thing—and at deep discounts, too. The inventories they offer are likely to be limited to jackets that come only in bright orange instead of blue or just in size 10, but the savings transform these shopping centers into a retailer-sanctioned treasure hunt. The secondary market should be viewed the same way. Companies should consider creating authorized resellers and dropshops for their products in order to control distribution and maintain their brands. Customers will get the same service and authenticity they would expect from walking out of an outlet store with bulging bags.

There are many ways to create authorized channels. Some companies have incorporated the exchange format directly into their own Web sites. Remember the discussion of Amazon and the thought that the company was cannibalizing a bit of itself to sell used books? Starting in late 2000, Amazon began listing used books next to new ones. Publishers grumbled and authors begged the company to give its new books more attention instead. Remember the book *Blown to Bits,* which warned us about ignoring technological innovation? New copies of the book sell through Amazon for around eighteen dollars, while Amazon itself posts listings alongside its exchange where independent sellers ask less than one dollar for it. A few interested buyers will probably select the cheaper version of this particular piece of merchandise, but Amazon is both participating in the transaction and keeping its customer. Amazon's move let the company stay competitive; revenues have soared over the last three years to nearly $7 billion in 2004. Used books clearly weren't responsible for all of that, but analysts did credit third-party sellers, including resellers, with helping Amazon exceed Wall Street expectations in 2005.

The bottom line: companies that don't endorse a secondary-market channel partner or partners for their products will find their products trading in an unruly way. When they do endorse an official channel partner, customers who love their brand will either buy or sell through that venue, ensuring consistency in service and quality that is in line with the brand.

Initiate Trade-In and Upgrade Programs

The *New York Times* reported in 2004 that American retailers tend to get stuck with $80 billion worth of overstock and returned inventory every year. For companies who are, for their own reasons, loath to see their products sold in the auction marketplace at all, a smart tactic is to offer customers a reason to keep those products out of the secondary market.

The main idea behind a trade-in program is for a company to control the supply of its product as well as to ensure the loyalty of a customer who has already adopted the brand. A large part of what allows the secondary market to thrive is the existence of goods in the market, and if those products come back to their home base, then the company itself can control more of the supply. In some situations, destroying these products may be an economically sound choice if having them in the marketplace can have negative consequences for a specific brand. Some companies already do this, driven by concern that discounting their goods will hurt their image and dilute their brand. Louis Vuitton and Hermès, for example, have indicated that they shred and incinerate their unsold goods. Other companies, especially in the consumer electronics industry, encourage businesses and individual consumers to return their products for refurbishment. Those products sometimes end up being donated in bulk to people who need them, especially groups in the public sector, such as schools.

The key to this method of controlling supply is to offer customers incentives to return the products to the place where they bought them when the products no longer have value to them. This can be done through programs that encourage customers to trade in or upgrade.

New products are coming out all the time. It makes sense to capitalize on that. Imagine if a regular customer could bring designer clothing back to a high-end department store, get credit, and then buy a new look from the same label. In other words, these products would never even reach a dropshop because they would come back to their brand owner through a lucrative in-house program. For some companies that are concerned with the exclusivity of their brand, this could be a way to keep products out of the secondary market instead of resorting to using overly aggressive tactics such as pulling legitimate auctions from online exchanges like eBay.

Whether it's clothing, computers, golf clubs, or cell phones, the benefits of instituting a trade-in program are the same: you are able to more closely monitor your supply in the secondary market, you give the customer a reason to come back to your authorized channel, and you ensure that your customer stays with your brand. It's a very powerful proposition that is already beginning to be adopted by the mainstream brand owners and retailers. Overall, auction culture should have a positive effect on businesses that can intelligently anticipate it.

Future-minded consumer electronics retailer Circuit City created an experimental trade-in and dropshop business in 2004 called Trading Circuit, starting with several storefronts in Atlanta and then opening additional test stores in Pittsburgh. It seemed like a solid plan. The storefronts would be annexed to Circuit City retail stores where there was already extra space due to a shift to self-service, or they would be set up in the company's unused warehouses. Circuit City hoped the side business would also bring in revenue by taking a cut of the profit whenever items processed through the dropshop sold on eBay. Customers could come to Trading Circuit stores with their unwanted items and Trading Circuit employees would take it from there, managing the auction process. When the dropshop model turned out to be too different from the company's core business to justify the resources required, Circuit City retooled its approach and forged an online trade-in program accessible through its Web site. Customers can now find out how much their used electronics are worth, send them back to Circuit City, and get a gift card for the final amount. On the back end, Circuit City still uses eBay to sell the items. For companies like Circuit City, eBay has become a boon for unloading consumer electronics that would otherwise have to be liquidated at far lower prices.

Technological heavyweight Hewlett-Packard created a trade-in program for a wide range of products, including printers, digital cameras, and PDAs. The program came into being in part because of environmental concerns over discarded products, but has also evolved to provide an effective solution to an electronics-specific problem. Checking the trade-in value of an old piece of computer equipment has the potential to be a sharp reality check. Customers tend to think that their gadgets are worth more than they actually are. The constant forward pulse of technology means that electronic devices can lose their value quickly. Despite the decline, HP does let customers put trade-in value towards a new purchase. In some cases, HP offers its customers more to trade in a model—such as an old Canon PowerShot—than an eager seller can get through an eBay auction. Customers are inevitably going to seek the most they can get for their old stuff, so an ideal trade-in program will be sure to offer good value. And even if the HP product no longer has any value in the consumer marketplace, the company will still take it back. In 2004, HP made it simpler for small and medium-sized businesses to trade in their old "Y2K ready" computers by offering discounts and rebates. The following year, eBay and Intel started a program with a host of other major computing retailers, including HP, Apple, and Dell, as well as government and environmental organizations, to consolidate their computer recycling efforts. The Rethink program offers consumers a source for finding ways to get rid of their old equipment through a site hosted by eBay.

A continuous trade-in program is also one way to satisfy customers' quests for a good deal. Picture a company that makes personal digital assistants and has customers who always have to have the latest version of a PDA as soon as it hits stores. Predictably, those same customers will want the newest model the following year, and the year after that, and every subsequent year. Why not incorporate that acquisitiveness into the product itself and ensure fidelity in the process? Loyal customers could be given an opportunity to enroll in a trade-in program for a set period of, say, five years. The program gives customers reasonable prices in exchange for their loyalty; they can trade in their old PDAs at regular intervals for the next newest version.

This proposed strategy hasn't matured yet in the consumer goods markets, but it has been implemented by a number of software companies that employ it to encourage customers to continue buying their product, using discounts on upgrades as incentives. Taken to a logical conclusion, this approach should lead to a whole new relationship between consumers and products: customers can be encouraged to buy a brand for the long haul, rather than just a specific item. That means that customers will have access to the latest model as soon as it comes out. In fact, subscribers could be given a chance to get products before they're even available to the general public, developing brand exclusivity. This can also be an effective technique for building momentum for a new product line: customers can trade in products they bought two or three years earlier and use that credit to purchase an exciting new product from the same company.

Companies can even make some money by reselling these returned products in the secondary-goods marketplace. Take California-based Dealtree.com, for example, which bills itself on its Web site as "a provider of returns management, product testing services, and disposal of returned, discontinued, and over-stocked merchandise." Internet retailers Paul Fletcher and Garry Heath noticed that hulking retailers in the consumer electronics sector lacked efficient ways to dispose of returned and obsolete inventory, Fletcher told Knight Ridder news service. They came up with Dealtree to step in and help with the problem. Dealtree's trade-in estimator will tell you what they (and their affiliates) will pay for an item to be traded in, including the shipping to them. For example, typing in "Blackberry 7100" yields a result of $89.99. Curiously, the same used PDA/phone trades on eBay for about $175 and is very liquid. Its easy to figure out that Dealtree can double its money by selling the product you trade in with them on eBay!

Beyond reselling, another strategy is to take returned products and channel them to poor communities in other countries, where the products can be redistributed at a fraction of the price without disturbing the prime markets. Computers for Africa, a nonprofit based in Nebraska, is one such organization that does just that. Since its inception, the organization has sent literally tons of computers overseas.

Used in conjunction, trade-in and upgrade programs not only help manufacturers control the secondary market, but they also give customers incentives to trade up more frequently. The trade-in-and-up strategy can lock customers in for years to come—giving them access to the next best style and the next best product—and those customers will come to identify with products in deeper, more profound ways than they would if they simply bought an individual item and took it home. With such programs, customers are less prone to turn to the secondary market because they've already purchased the next five versions of a product.

Track Secondary-Market Metrics

The resale market can also be used as a powerful market-research tool.

Every mature company should already have the capacity to track what happens to its products in the primary market, given the fact that point-of-sale data is one of the most valuable indicators as to how products are selling. Retailers live by it and manufacturers fight to get their hands on it. One of the biggest by-products of auction culture is that similar information is now available in the secondary market, too. In fact, the information is so rich, and—because the secondary market is so dominated by third parties—so transparent, that the data can be used not only to track the market for your own products, but to see what's happening with the competition's products as well.

In order to follow products in the secondary market, companies that aim to stay ahead of the curve will want to either leverage existing tracking tools or create the tools themselves. It's important to know how much your products trade for in the secondary market as well as how many of them are up for sale at any given point in time. After all, the way a company's product sells in the secondary market has a significant impact on how that company's products sell in the primary market. There is a strong correlation between the price for something new and the same thing used. The more valuable a product is, and the more residual value it retains in the secondary market, the more it can garner in the primary market. If a handbag is selling for $1,000 new and for $600 used, but then all of a sudden the used version begins trading at $800, the door is open for the company that makes it to introduce its next pocketbook at $1,200.

Tracking secondary-market data can be a powerful tool to recognize a challenge to primary sales. If a brand's value declines in the secondary market, that fact is immediately visible and requires a strategic response. Take the market for books as an example of how secondary-market data tells a story. A quick scan of books trading on the leading book exchanges, Half.com, Barnes & Noble, and Amazon, indicates a clear relationship between the type of book and the strength of its price in the secondary market. Reference books maintain the greatest value in the secondary market—a testament to their future usability. Fiction, in contrast, is generally read for entertainment and in most cases has limited value after a single read. Accordingly, its value declines quickly and is reflected as such in the secondary market. Popular fiction titles that retail for $29 new are available used and in perfect condition for a fraction of that price.

The following chart demonstrates the disparity in the new and used prices of three different books available at the same time on all three of the major exchanges. As the stigma associated with buying used books dissipates in the wake of auction culture, publishers will be increasingly challenged with this segment of their business. After all, though many avid readers like to keep lots of books on their bookshelves, others have neither the space nor the inclination to keep books they have little or no intention of revisiting. Using secondary-market data will help publishers to track the impact of used-book sales as they grow and to make necessary adjustments in their pricing or in the number of books they print.

Understanding the Relationship between Secondary Market Values and the Variables That Influence the Primary Markets

Title	Used	New	Savings	Type	Qty. Avail
Freakonomics	$11.00	$15.57	29%	Knowledge	85
Da Vinci Code	$6.00	$14.97	60%	Entertainment	807
Super System	$16.95	$19.77	17%	Reference	134

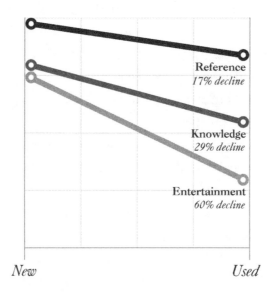

Reference
17% decline

Knowledge
29% decline

Entertainment
60% decline

New   *Used*

Secondary-market data can fill in the gaps in primary market data because the data isn't being kept secret in the way that primary-market data is withheld by most companies. EBay has been selling its data for more than a year now, and it is available to anyone willing to buy it. Other marketplaces are certain to follow and profit from making their data available as well. There are already a number of companies that track and manipulate this data for businesses that are interested in it, so that they don't have to build the tools themselves from scratch. (We'll get to those in the next chapter.) It's out there, just waiting to be interpreted: data on who is buying what, where they're buying it, and when—all in real time!

On any given day, for example, more than $250,000 of Apple iPod-related products sell on eBay. Armed with that information, competitors can determine Apple's market size, its performance relative to a prior period, and how fast the segment is growing (or not). They can plot the daily sales data for Apple products on a graph and observe the movements of price, supply, and demand in real time. What versions sell well? Which geographic regions are home to buyers most interested in the product? What colors are most popular? By developing appropriate algorithms to track the relationship between the secondary and primary markets, analysts can trade on this information well before Apple reports its sales. Retailers can stock up on the hottest products based on this information. And competitors can use this data to manage their own products as well.

A quirk in the secondary data can also be a sign of a change in the primary-market business of a competitor that would be empowering to know about. If there is a sudden spike in sales volume or average price, you want to understand the trigger as soon as possible. It could be a signal for other companies to take a look at that market. For example, if a particular flat-screen TV model drops in price dramatically one day, it might be a signal that the model is soon to become obsolete and a new one is coming out any moment. The price drop may actually reflect distributors dumping inventory, cautioning retailers to wait until more information comes from the manufacturer before committing to purchasing more inventory. This type of information has taken days, weeks, and months to disseminate in the past. In the near future, however, the reaction will be similar to stockbrokers' dumping stock in the market as they get early feeds of bad news being released by a company. Usually, companies have to wait a quarter or a year to get industry data, and it is never very detailed. In fact, in some categories, the manufacturers can't even get hard sales data from their own distributors or retailers.

Secondary-market data can also help companies make more informed decisions about product life cycles: when to discontinue an old model, when to introduce something new, how to time it. Say you're a cell phone manufacturer with an eye on the secondary market. All of a sudden the value of your latest, greatest cell phone model bottoms out. Last month it was selling for $180, then it rose to $200, and then it suddenly dropped to $50. Clearly, buyers aren't valuing your top-of-the-line phone anymore. What's going on? If consumers are dumping your best model, but they can't be trading up to a better one that you make—because it doesn't exist on the market yet—then there must be an explanation. Perhaps they are unloading your phone to buy a new one from a different manufacturer. If you were planning to wait to release your next phone model, you'll probably want to stop waiting and start making it available.

In general, many factors go into when to release a product. This is another factor that should be considered whenever a company is developing a product release strategy. Think back to those Nintendo scalpers in Chapter 6. By offering a game console at a higher price to customers desperate to find one, they actually helped maintain customer loyalty for Nintendo. Without the scalpers, frustrated customers likely would have bought some other brand instead. When it's possible to judge product sales in the secondary marketplace, it's easier to craft an informed business strategy for products in the retail market.

. . .

As you can see from these strategic insights, there are numerous ways that businesses can begin to prepare for change and start to embrace auction culture. Many emerging businesses are poised to flourish in this new world. Their creative takes on auction culture position them to help traditional businesses adapt to the new environment and capitalize on many of these insights. Remember when shopping online was new and slightly intimidating? Now it's the norm. The next generation of facilitators will make it just as easy to participate in auction culture. Get ready.

9 THE EVOLUTION OF A NEW ECOSYSTEM

Tomorrow's Opportunities

In each step of eBay's evolution, entrepreneurs have devised solutions to problems that have confronted users. When the secondary market emerged online ten years ago, one of the first companies that arrived on the scene to support it was PayPal. Like eBay itself, PayPal had humble beginnings, in a classroom on California's Stanford University campus, where a hedge fund manager named Peter Thiel was giving a lecture on international finance in the fall of 1998. Following his talk, a twenty-three-year-old Ukrainian émigré named Max Levchin approached Thiel to discuss an idea he had to create an encryption system to transfer information securely from one handheld computer to another. To make it commercially viable, Thiel tapped into his finance background and suggested that they focus on money exchange, according to Eric Jackson's book *The PayPal Wars*.

The pair's idea was originally to turn Palm Pilots and similar gadgets into portable automatic teller machines. They created a secure Web site to support their venture, which they called Confinity. Levchin was highly focused on maintaining security, especially since previous digital-cash ventures had failed by forcing the merchants to download encryption systems themselves. He also wanted to build a service that actively fought against fraud to solidify its users' trust, but the business initially struggled to gain recognition in a business climate already swirling with skepticism about digital-cash start-ups. Several similar ventures had already tanked. Confinity's Web site, PayPal.com, held the most promise, so the pioneers eventually decided to broaden their concept by relaunching their venture in November 1999 under the PayPal name. Using this service, people can send or receive payments through the site, which taps into their bank accounts or credit card accounts for the funds. Basic personal accounts are free, but the higher-level premier and business accounts give the user a way to accept credit or debit cards, and PayPal takes a small percentage whenever the account holders receive funds. PayPal also charges when overseas banks are involved.

To pull in as many users as possible after PayPal's debut, Thiel and Levchin offered the service for free and even handed out $10 credits (later $5) to anyone who signed up, or even to anyone who got other people to become registered users. PayPal could have become yet another defunct dot-com, except that it started to become useful to the ever-growing eBay community, which was continuously looking for easier and safer ways to transact. Later, Thiel and Levchin would admit that they had never considered their product for the consumer secondary market when they first launched. The service they provided, however, was so well suited to online consumer-to-consumer transactions, allowing buyers and sellers to exchange money instantly, that it quickly became as mainstream as using a credit card in a department store.

PayPal became the quintessential first-generation business to piggyback on the online auction phenomenon and helped partners like eBay grow rapidly by providing a solution to one of the new business's unique challenges—working out a secure and reliable method by which payments could be made and received. Before PayPal, according to *Technology Review*, 90 percent of all transactions conducted through eBay were accomplished by check, which could take up to ten days to travel and then clear. Most users didn't have the ability to accept credit cards and had no interest in investing either the time or the cost to establish accounts. But by July 2000, about two million eBay listings carried the PayPal logo, meaning that sellers were encouraging buyers to pay through the secure online site. EBay had its own rival payment program, Billpoint, but it was less sophisticated and less popular than PayPal. Soon, PayPal had completely overshadowed Billpoint, which was consequently phased out. Now eBay owns PayPal, which it bought for $1.5 billion in stock. The move, which effectively nullified the competition between the two forces, paid off formidably, as PayPal now generates nearly 30 percent of eBay's revenue, according to *Barron's*.

Assuring that financial transactions were both simple and secure was a major turning point for online secondary markets. But as the system evolved, new issues continued to emerge. Though eBay set up its VeRO program to assist companies in verifying the authenticity of goods being offered for sale, the risk of buying a fake, damaged, or misrepresented product was, and still is, a serious concern for eBay users. Lots of buyers are skeptical. How can you really know for sure what you're getting? Once again, entrepreneurial thinking addressed the issues. A Southern California–based company called Escrow.com started in 1999 offering buyers a PayPal alternative: instead of sending money directly to the unknown seller, Escrow.com acts as a trusted depository to ensure that the goods a buyer has won are exactly how the seller has described them before the transaction is concluded. The parties agree on a period of time that the buyer has to inspect the item, and the buyer maintains the right to reject the item and arrange for it to be returned if it's found to be less than represented. Escrow also offers an automated feature called TransactionPoint that uses third-party services to track each step that goes into an online transaction, including the exchange of funds and the creation of binding legal contracts. "Our primary focus is to become the trusted third party," David Sklar, Escrow's former chief financial officer, told *Computer Reseller News* in October 2000. "In the offline world, there's a lot of complexity in doing financial transactions with someone. And they don't go away in the online world."

A company called SquareTrade, founded in 1999, became another beam in the online auction scaffolding. As e-commerce expanded (particularly across borders), conflict resolution between buyers and sellers became a necessity, especially given the reluctance of so many online marketplaces to mediate. SquareTrade resolves disputes between buyers and sellers online, acting as their de facto arbitrator, in exchange for a nominal fixed fee plus a percentage of the transaction under review. Since its inception, SquareTrade has forged partnerships with eBay, Yahoo!, and other online exchanges.

Soon, others joined SquareTrade. *Entrepreneur* magazine published an April 2002 article urging readers to use online mediators such as ClickNsettle.com, Cybersettle.com, OnlineResolution.com, and WebMediate.com, as well as SquareTrade. "When a deal made over the Internet goes sour, it may be harder to resolve the problem than when you're dealing with people face to face," the article noted. "Chances are you're dealing with an entity you don't know, most likely located in some far away legal jurisdiction. Commercial law varies some from state to state, and much more from country to country." The new crop of companies proved that wherever there were barriers to using online auctions effectively, solutions could be found.

Just as these services were developed to respond to issues that arose as eBay evolved, more and more innovative services will be cropping up to proactively support the growing auction culture. A look at the new generation of companies that have already started emerging shows how wide a variety of opportunities there will be. Some of these companies are approaching adolescence, others are in their infancies, a few exist only on the horizon, and some are destined to become major players in the new consumer culture.

Individual consumers and large companies alike will embrace these businesses, which will help facilitate, protect, monitor, and manage product transactions in this new market. Let's take a look at what the future could hold.

RIDING THE WAVE

The hottest business segment to emerge so far has been the auction facilitator, with dropshops leading the way. This breed of new business will appear as a staple service in every community within the next few years—as ubiquitous as dry cleaners, service stations, and Starbucks. But, like brick-and-mortar businesses such as auction houses, thrift shops, and pawnbrokers, auction culture facilitators will be as diverse as the items that flow through eBay every day.

As we're already seeing, some facilitators will focus on high-end products while others will compete for cheaper items by providing a generic, basic, no-frills service. Expect more genre-specific drop-shops, too. For example, Auction123, based in Fort Lauderdale, Florida, is an eBay Motors–based dropshop and listing service specifically for cars that caters to both dealers and consumers.

The advent of new kinds of leasing models for a variety of products will probably be next on the evolutionary ladder of the auction culture. There is already a company cleverly named Bag Borrow or Steal that lets Carrie Bradshaw types lease the hottest designer handbags. Operating like the Netflix of the luxury hand-bag world, Bag Borrow or Steal customers pay a monthly fee to, essentially, rent handbags according to their needs. The company's business model lets patrons join the service at a variety of levels, which dictate the brand names they can access. As of 2005, you could start at the Trendsetter level for $19.95 per month and choose Cynthia Rowley and Kate Spade bags, whereas members of the Diva Deluxe level, at $174.95 per month, paid for the priv-ilege of draping Valentino, Versace, and Tod's bags on their arms. Every member can borrow unlimited numbers of bags per month for unlimited amounts of time (as long as the member is in good standing), but all shipping and handling fees are additional. At whatever level they join, though, members are getting access to many models and colors that are no longer available through retail channels. Eventually, there will be hundreds of companies like Bag Borrow or Steal—one for every drool-inducing item worth keeping until a new one appears.

Bag Borrow or Steal has even started to address one of the other new key issues that will confront this kind of leasing business: insurance. For an extra few bucks, members can purchase insurance to cover excessive wear and tear on the bags, although it doesn't cover theft or loss—if that happens, members are charged a replacement fee. But, like the in-house special insurance program, a new genre of insurance companies will grow popular as we seek to protect our items against wear and tear, and even against the loss of purchases like cell phones and shoes that we bought with the intention of reselling in a year's time. Today, collectibles-specific insurance companies like InsureCollectibles.com are filling pieces of this market, but in the future this type of insurance won't just be reserved for arrowheads and pens.

On the buyer's side, there's a different kind of insurance that makes it safer to shop, adding to a base of services that eBay and PayPal offer. While he was interning at a technology company in 2000, Steve Woda had a bad buying experience on eBay when he tried to purchase a handheld computer. It left him without his money and handheld, too, so he dreamed up BuySAFE as a way to fight fraud. Sellers go through an application process with the company, and trustworthy sellers get a seal of approval in exchange for a 1 percent commission on sales. Then their transactions are guaranteed through BuySAFE's surety bond agreement with Liberty Mutual. If the seller doesn't deliver, buyers can be reimbursed for purchases up to $25,000.

As the auction culture develops, the increased availability of good-quality used items may actually even help to lower the costs of traditional insurance. Currently, if a hurricane splinters a house or a fire scorches an apartment, insurance is meant to cover replacement costs—the price you'd have to pay for new versions of all your belongings. In the future, when the market is much more liquid, you'll more likely be able to find the exact used versions of your bedside table, your dish collection, and your favorite comfy chair. The insurance company will save money, and that savings will be passed on to their customers in their premium payments.

Another approach to the problem of damaged goods is the warranty. Companies that offer warranties for secondhand goods will provide another kind of safeguard for auction culture shoppers. National Electronics Warranty Corporation, or NEW, originally founded in 1983, has long managed service contracts and product warranties. Now the company sells warranties for eBay customers, guaranteeing products bought in the secondary market and eliminating the risk of getting stuck holding the bill for a defective product. Like insurance, the warranty plans are priced according to the item and its retail cost. Usually the company provides warranties for things like watches and consumer electronics. NEW's partnership with eBay produced a service agreement that users can purchase. It covers parts and labor, comes with 24/7 customer service, and if any item requires more than three repairs for the same thing, NEW will replace it for free. More such companies will probably appear as the auction culture booms.

PERSONAL ASSISTANCE

As the concept of continually culling our wardrobes and replacing our possessions catches on, a whole new breed of lifestyle consultants will emerge to advise us on when and what to buy and sell. From personal assistants to feng shui experts, these specialists will help us recognize when our things are approaching their expiration dates.

Feng shui expert Anita Rosenberg sees a major opportunity in the auction culture lifestyle. Rosenberg runs her own feng shui business, applying her knowledge to homes, offices, and commercial spaces like restaurants. "For new opportunities to come calling, you need space—physical space in your closet," Rosenberg advises. And since feng shui equates money with energy, Rosenberg believes that the impetus auction culture provides to clean out our physical spaces and get remuneration for it is a perfect catalyst for personal improvement. "If you think about it from a feng shui point of view," Rosenberg said, "eBay is really just moving energy around." As auction culture catches on and more individuals start to think about living a more balanced and efficient life with their belongings, her business is poised to enjoy a surge in popularity.

Julie Subotky was a personal assistant in Aspen, Colorado, for many years, helping clients who didn't have enough time to get through their daily to-do lists. Subotky didn't blink when assigned tasks like addressing five thousand Christmas cards, coordinating travel for clients, and even managing large events like weddings and benefits. But when she found herself settling into New York City, she discovered a whole clientele of people whose to-do lists were crammed to the max. She started her own business, called Consider it Done, and her philosophy has been to say yes and then work through the "how" part. "I think there's so much going on in people's everyday lives that people have a long list of things to do," she said. "We like to do it as if they've done it . . . like a little elf came in."

As a personal assistance company, one of Consider it Done's

more frequent requests is to manage moves and home renovations for clients, overseeing various vendors and making sure all the boxes go where they are supposed to. Through the home-purging process, Subotky got to see plenty of boxes that hadn't been opened for, well, longer than her clients could even remember. Sometimes there was a musty collection that clients forgot that they even had—baseball cards or an old dollhouse. When confronted, some clients sheepishly hoped that they might someday be passed on to future generations. But the vast majority of the time, "It's not worth it," Subotky says. "It might take someone like us in the house to say, 'Are you really going to use it?'" Fifteen years ago she would have told her clients to donate it. Now she can say, "Let's just sell it," and clients will be even more likely to take her advice. "I want my clients to have every benefit that they can, and I think eBay culture makes it a lot easier for people in general," she says. Consider it Done and similar personal assistance services are already becoming the new hot business and will further benefit from the emergence of auction culture as they come up with creative ways to unearth value for their clients in this new world.

Professional closet creators and organizers will also come to the rescue. Melanie Charlton makes it her business to be in other people's closets. Her company, Clos-ette, designs high-end closet spaces, organizes belongings for clients, and then maintains the space over time with careful "edits," as Charlton calls them. Clos-ette, known to many as the "closet company to the stars," has become increasingly dependent on eBay to sell clients' unwanted items, thereby playing a key role in the auction culture facilitation process, both utilizing and popularizing the service to a clientele that's less likely to come to it on their own. Today her company is a Portero affiliate and exclusively uses Portero to get maximum value for her clients' previously owned fashion. It used to be that Charlton had only a few choices when clients found couture that no longer fit or vintage handbags they no longer carried: consignment or charity. Now, when she uncovers two-year-old Prada shoes or a twenty-year-old Oleg Cassini dress, she can arrange to have them sold on eBay and other online channels through Portero. "I see the future of my business being very lucrative," Charlton says. As luxury becomes increasingly accessible through the new auction culture, professionals will need more editing help to keep their closets fresh. "Closets are no longer the forgotten child of the house," she says. "They're very much up there with the kitchen and the bathroom." Charlton's core value proposition is editing your life so that your wardrobe is always current. As more and more consumers embrace the notion of letting go of clothing they no longer wear sooner and sooner, Charlton's business will benefit and other such companies will surely emerge.

Another innovative service that will come in handy for auction culture mavens is the clothing storage company. Along with closet organizers and editors, clothing storage and inventory services are poised to profit from shoppers' new outlooks. Kim Akhtar, a professional flamenco dancer and executive coordinating producer for the CBS *Evening News,* discovered the clothing storage scarcity in New York City the hard way. Tight on space, she left her bulky winter clothes with the dry cleaner for a season. It turned out to be a move that cost her $10,000 when she went to pick it all up. Akhtar realized that other New Yorkers, prone to turning unused ovens into shoe caddies, were struggling for space, too, so she created a storage and virtual valet company called Garde Robe (French for "wardrobe"). Garde Robe cata-logs and stores clothing and accessories in a Manhattan loft, giv-ing clients remote online access to their virtual closets as well as quick delivery when the items are needed. You can see what you have—whether it's in the loft or hanging on the back of your door—just by looking on a computer. Eventually, when more of these virtual closets take off, anyone will be able to edit their own closets and decide in a flash what to unload on eBay. In a crammed closet, pieces are out of sight and out of mind. With everything laid out on the computer, Garde Robe facilitates the timely tran-sition of the items you aren't using efficiently.

Glimpsing a potential extension of their business, Akhtar and her partners recently set up a small online consignment shop on the Garde Robe Web site. "The minute you say, 'Let me do it,' you see instant relief on their faces," Akhtar said. At first, Garde Robe had only three pairs of shoes to sell, but now business is brisk and the number of hits the consignment store site receives is consistently going up. Castoffs from "maybe" clothing piles quickly find new homes and relieved clients pocket the proceeds. As of 2005, Garde Robe charges at least $150 an hour for such a service, but as the market grows, this type of help will become more financially accessible.

Not only do clothing services help to keep track of the items you own, they also help keep them in good shape. Storing your clothes with services like Garde Robe will help preserve clothing quality and preserve the resale value of those belongings.

Even traditional storage companies are realizing that auction culture is part of their future. One might consider it counterintu-itive that a traditional storage company would want to see clients selling their stuff—after all, doesn't that reduce the amount of storage space they can rent them? But that's not the case. Historically, people have never had the opportunity to distinguish between storing something they want but have no space for or storing something that they really never want to see again but feel guilty about throwing away. With the auction culture at our doorstep, mini-storage facilities are facing the reality of where our culture is moving, and some of the more innovative ones are taking an aggressive and cutting-edge step by becoming the first-movers in recognizing the added value they can deliver to their customers.

Manhattan Mini Storage, the largest mini-storage company in New York City, with almost forty thousand units and customers, recently aligned with Portero to provide their clients with a method to dispose of unwanted valuables that clutter their storage units—before they move in, while they are there, and before they leave. MMS markets itself as an extension of your home where you can keep the things you want to keep but can't quite accommodate in your tight Manhattan apartment. The company's fresh advertising campaign features chic Manhattanites storing their winter-related possessions like skis and parkas in their "closet away from home" so they have more room for their summer belongings. Portero will maintain a presence at each of its thirteen facilities to help clients edit their storage units as needed and sell their unwanted items online. Manhattan Mini Storage sees this as a way to add much more value to customers than renting them storage units bigger than they really need. And in the end, the goodwill pays off with happy customers who feel good about their storage service.

Even if you don't use a storage facility, city dwellers are soon to see the subtle but clear signs of auction culture permeating their lives wherever they live. The Related Companies, one of New

York's largest luxury apartment building developers, recently integrated Portero into every one of their six thousand apartment units. When you want something out of your life, just pick up your house phone and dial 6-2-2. You can even leave your valuables with the doorman for Portero to pick up while you are at work. Jeff Blau, Related's president, predicts that in-house dropshop services will become as ubiquitous as the concierge service they have in each of their buildings: "We are about bringing the leading types of services to our tenants and are usually the first to offer what eventually becomes ubiquitous among luxury buildings."

RESTORING VALUE

There are always services we can employ to get first-class treatment for our clothes, but what about scuffs on shoes? Broken purse straps? Scratches on an iPod? Since few of these have traditionally been considered value-retaining items, we haven't needed to maintain them diligently. But as we embrace temporary ownership, we'll need a diverse range of restorers to smooth the daily wear and tear from the surfaces of our belongings. Companies that can handle a wide range of these requests will be in great demand.

There are other ways to restore value to items you might be looking to resell. Today, you keep the bulky boxes that products come in until you know for sure that they work. Then it ends up in the trash (or the recycling bin). But the right packaging goes a long way to make a "used" item feel more "like new." Imagine buying a spare box for the brand new plasma-screen television at the register when you make your initial purchase, letting the company store it for you, and then having it sent to you later, when you're ready to sell or trade in the TV. Packaging services won't just be limited to consumer electronics, they'll extend to anything that could use a box, and you'll even be able to order a duplicate copy of whatever instruction manuals a future owner might want to be thrown in.

Other assistance will come from companies like PartSearch. com, which provides replacement parts for consumer electronics. This type of service adds value to used items. Say, for example, that you want to sell a TV, but you don't have the original remote. PartSearch can get it for you. Or perhaps your cell phone or PDA has a defective battery. Instead of trying to unload it that way, you can replace the battery first. Retailers including RadioShack, Best Buy, and CompUSA also rely on PartSearch to provide this service for their customers.

The future won't just be about caring for and cataloging clothes and accessories, but doing the same for anything you want to store—or perhaps every last thing you own. You'll be able to stay on top of what you use and what you don't, and then get help selling whatever is going stale. Do-it-yourself types can already check eBay trends to find out what their collectibles are worth through sites like SmartCollector.com, which also lets you track purchases from eBay with a portfolio manager that can show the current value range for each item. Soon, other entrepreneurs will launch similar sites for wide ranges of noncollectibles.

As auction culture takes hold, we'll also see a rise in the number of authenticators who can assure us of our products' pedigrees. Web sites have already sprung up all over, cobbled together by both experts and concerned shopaholics, with advice on how to tell the difference between a fake and the real deal. Take IHate-CounterfeitBags.info, which instructs Kate Spade fans on how to instantly spot rip-offs. MyPoupette.com does the same for Louis Vuitton and also warns visitors about specific LV scams on eBay.

Beyond these antifakery grassroots watchdog groups, legitimate authentication services that have traditionally built up around collectibles and antiques will be in increasingly high demand for everyday items like shoes, clothing, and sports equipment. These services will tap into networks of authorized appraisers to get the job done. Large companies will be able to provide this type of service themselves. Remember the authentication systems from the last chapter? That technology will help companies maintain searchable databases of all their uniquely identified wares.

Virtual appraisers are already starting to attract attention. To find out what your cell phone is worth, just ask the people at WhatsItWorthToYou.com, an appraisal hub for eBay. Basic appraisals cost around $5 to $8 per item; you access them by submitting a question to appraisal experts via a form on the site. One of the supplemental services that WhatsItWorthToYou offers is called The Security Exchange, an extra layer of security that allows you to have a seller send your purchases through their appraisers first, to make sure the items are exactly what the seller has described, before they are sent on to you.

On the business-to-business side, we'll see a host of new companies emerge to support the change in consumer behavior. Already scores of businesses offer consulting services for eBay stores, providing "expert" assistance with areas such as listing design and customer service. In April 2004, eBay harnessed this trend and set up a formal certification program to recognize companies with proven records that embrace eBay's platform. These companies tend to be service providers that have come up with helpful tools such as customized software for businesses that want to maximize their presence on eBay.

On the consumer side, services that used to be reserved only for businesses will soon be increasingly available in relevant forms to individual sellers. Take eBay-recommended Dependable Auto Shippers, which specializes in moving vehicles cross-country and to other countries. If the need to get something large from point A to point B is what's stopping you from taking advantage of the secondary market, there will soon be an assortment of services popping up to help you get it done. After all, it's easy to transact with buyers and sellers on the other side of the world using the Internet, but it's still the other side of the world. We haven't quite reached the point where we can "beam" objects from sellers to buyers yet. Until we do, there will be an increasing number of facilitators that cut down on the time and hassle involved in sending a piece of furniture from Australia to America. The Canadian company A & A Custom Contract Brokers has been around since 1979, but has evolved into a focused eBay facilitator, assisting importers and exporters with "cross-border and international shipping, customs brokerage, warehousing, and distribution." Businesses like this will ease the complexities inherent in transglobal trade. In no time, you'll be able to seamlessly buy a leather massaging chair from Australia the way you would from someone in the next town over in America.

AUCTIONS AS ENTERTAINMENT

In 2005, Time Warner introduced "eBay on TV," an interactive subscription service that lets channel surfers use eBay from their couches, and Bonfire Media created a way to use eBay from mobile phones. Auctions are everywhere now, and no media sector wants to be left out of the party. EBay is live on the radio waves with its own online station, "eBay Radio," where founder Pierre

Omidyar does a fireside chat, Meg Whitman shares a keynote address, and eBay personality "Uncle Griff" interviews eBay insiders and responds to caller's questions.

Ambitious producers are already developing television shows to ride the online auction explosion, introducing programs similar to the successful PBS series *Antiques Roadshow,* which goes from town to town valuing possessions hauled in by hordes of hopeful prospectors. AuctionDrop recently started airing a weekly half-hour segment on cable TV in Northern California that highlighted the "coolest" items being offered for sale that week. The Discovery Channel got in on the act, too, with *Pop Nation,* a reality-TV series that has experts appraise items gathered by die-hard pop-culture collectors. The participants face a tough choice in the end: keep their precious items, sell them for a profit to an independent buyer, or wager them on eBay through a dropshop. We can be reasonably assured that we'll see even more reality TV invade the auction culture—like shows where families compete to create value from their unused possessions. And you can be certain that eventually a lifestyle guru will emerge—a Martha Stewart–like personality who proselytizes on the art of living well in the auction culture and who builds an empire from showing consumers how to do it with panache.

AN ECONOMIC JUGGERNAUT

As in all of life, knowledge will be power in the auction culture. Businesses that specialize in tracking secondary-market data, such as Andale and Terapeak, will be highly sought-after resources for just about everyone looking to profit from the new paradigm. They'll expand their base of clientele well beyond the small mom-and-pop businesses making a living on eBay, selling data to other new companies that will in turn design innovative economic models to harness the newfound buying power rampant in the new economy. Specifically, the dissemination of data by the exchanges and the power to manipulate it provided by the software companies will empower a variety of companies to operate with greater precision than they do today. Software company Andale, launched in 1999 with the backing of millions of venture capital dollars, created a blueprint for what information service providers stand to gain by catering to sellers who want to know what moves and what doesn't. Andale's software sifts through historical eBay auctions to divine the top sellers in various categories, which helps the buyers of that data to make more money by focusing on selling items with the greatest demand.

Brothers Andrew and Anthony Sukow also recognized how important it was to understand eBay's economics. In 2003, they formed a next-generation database company called Terapeak in Victoria, British Columbia, that licenses eBay's transaction data and offers it to subscribers, harnessing hundreds of millions of transactions in their interactive site. Other tools for understanding what's hot and what's not will emerge, allowing market-research firms specializing in analyzing this data to provide counsel and guidance to corporate America, whether as new businesses or new departments within large consulting firms.

. . .

WITH ALL THESE OPPORTUNITIES, there will be winners who ride the wave of change as well as losers who find themselves removed from the game, caught in a tug-of-war between the various players pulling in different directions. There is a power struggle taking place to define who is going to control the pace at which the new economy will take shape. The online exchanges are on one side, the brands and retailers on the other, and the consumers sit in between. The state of things is reminiscent of the early days of the Internet, when the traditional businesses lined up on one side and the facilitators and innovators on the other. Change was threatening then, just as it is now, to those who benefit from the status quo and who are afraid that they can't adapt to new ways of doing business. Order will eventually emerge as the new culture is broadly adopted and matures and naysayers realize that the change is for the better, and even in their own interest.

In our material world, society has a love-hate relationship with the principle of proactive self-interest, which suggests that in striving, selfishly, to do well for ourselves, we are actually most likely to do well for each other in the aggregate. But this basic tenet of capitalism indicates that as we as consumers act to minimize the costs and maximize the benefits of our acquisitions, we'll all live better and more cheaply than we did before—the simple result of a more efficient world. I don't have a crystal ball, and can't tell you exactly when it will happen, but when the auction culture revolution hits full stride, it will make the world a better place for everyone.

A NOTE ON THE DATA

Much of the data in this book is derived from quantitative research using information that was meticulously accumulated from many sources. The data was collected over the course of a year using various methodologies that included manual aggregation as well as proprietary technologies from public and private sources. A large portion of data comes directly from eBay (and its affiliates), which only recently provided access to its database of historical transactions conducted on the eBay.com Web site. Despite the transparency of data on the Internet as well as the ability to publicly access data licensed by eBay, there are still significant limitations in both the breadth and depth of the data. Specifically, much of the data is limited to transactions that originate in the United States. EBay also limits the types of searches that can occur on its data in a manner that protects itself from the peering eyes of Wall Street analysts, with their ability to use the data to predict eBay's operating performance in advance of its public reporting. These limitations required me to periodically combine pieces of related data from multiple sources to analyze markets and arrive at extrapolated conclusions. While this technique necessarily renders some of the underlying conclusions scientifically imperfect, the conclusions present an accurate view of the respective markets.

ACKNOWLEDGMENTS

Writing *FutureShop* was an adventure. The experience was fun, the task was challenging, and the actual work was exhausting. From start to finish, it required the direct and indirect help of many people.

I would like to first thank Jennifer Joel, literary agent extraordinaire and good friend. Jennifer's contribution was immense, and I am very fortunate to know her and have had her involved with this work.

I would like to also thank the many people who helped me along the way (in no specific order):

Emily Loose, William Mougayar, Bill Engles, Steve Kettmann, Alyssa Danigelis, Robert Kay, Howard Levitt, Stanley Greenstein, Michael Sheldon, Barbara Kolsun, Lisa Jacobs, Doris Meister, Owen Maher (graphics), and the many individuals who participated in interviews for the book.

Thanks to the entire Portero team for building a

platform that has helped me constantly refine many of the underlying concepts in this book.

Finally, I would like to thank my wife, Amy, and my son, Asher, for patiently allowing me the seemingly endless nights and weekends I needed to get to this point.

SELECTED REFERENCES

Bunnell, David with Richard A. Luecke. *The eBay Phenomenon: Business Secrets Behind the World's Hottest Internet Company.* John Wiley & Sons, Inc., New York, NY, 2000. (ISBN 0-471-38490-9)

Cohen, Adam. *The Perfect Store: Inside eBay.* Little, Brown, New York, NY, 2002. (ISBN 0-316-15048-7)

Evans, Philip and Thomas S. Wurster. *Blown to Bits: How the New Economics of Information Transforms Strategy.* Harvard Business School Press, Cambridge, MA, 1999. (ISBN 0-875-84877-X)

Flink, James J. *The Automobile Age.* MIT Press, Cambridge, MA, 1988. (ISBN 0-262-06111-2)

Genat, Robert. *The American Car Dealership.* MBI Publishing Company, Osceola, WI, 1999. (ISBN 0-7603-0639-7)

Harden, Leland and Bob Heyman. *The Auction-App: How Companies Tap the Power of Online Auctions to Maximize Growth.* McGraw-Hill, New York, NY, 2002. (ISBN 0-07-138735-8)

Learmount, Brian. *A History of the Auction.* Barnard & Learmount, Great Britain, 1985. (ISBN 0-9510240-0-0)

Perkins, Edwin J. *Wall Street to Main Street: Charles Merrill and Middle-Class Investors.* Cambridge University Press, Cambridge, United Kingdom, 1999. (ISBN 0-521-63029-0)

INDEX

ABOUT THE AUTHOR

Daniel Nissanoff is an entrepreneur who is an internationally recognized and accomplished expert in secondary-market economies, technologies, and businesses.

In 1994, the same year that eBay was founded, Nissanoff began focusing his professional energies on building a central online business-to-business exchange for the highly fragmented and inefficient electronic components industry. By the late 1990s, he had brought his vision to reality and founded a company called PartMiner. Working with a team of technologists from IBM's renowned Watson Research Center, Nissanoff built the "Free Trade Zone," a NASDAQ-like trading and information platform, which became one of the world's first business-to-business virtual marketplaces and the leading online marketplace for the semiconductor industry. Today, PartMiner's digital solutions are used by almost all of the top electronics manufacturers in the world, helping facilitate billions of dollars in trade.

While at PartMiner, Nissanoff invented the first commercially deployed business shopping robot, and he also holds various patents for marketplace technologies and business processes for the secondary market.

In 2004, having spent most of his professional life on the b2b sector, Nissanoff decided to dedicate the next phase to the consumer side of secondary markets. In addition to sharing his vision globally by writing this book, he has spent the last year helping to build Portero, a specialty online facilitator focused on the secondary market for luxury consumer products.

Nissanoff was a 2001 finalist for the coveted Ernst and Young Entrepreneur of the Year Award. He was named a "Mover and Shaker of 2001" by *Electronic Industry,* alongside fourteen CEOs of multi-billion-dollar public electronics companies. His deal with IBM was recognized by Line56 as one of the Top 20 Events in 2000. Under his leadership, PartMiner was ranked as a Deloitte Fast 500 company, for two years in a row. He is also an active member of Young President's Organization (YPO), an international assembly of over 11,000 influential business leaders, since 1999. He has been a frequent public speaker and featured guest at prominent events worldwide, including Internet seminars, venture capital workshops, semiconductor industry events, and platform user conferences. Hundreds of articles have been written about him, his companies, his views and cutting-edge strategies on the Internet.

Prior to conceiving PartMiner, Nissanoff founded a software company that automated secondary markets. Previously, he was also an associate attorney in the corporate reorganization group of the law firm of Weil, Gotshal and Manges.

Daniel Nissanoff holds a J.D. from New York University School of Law and a B.S. in Economics from California State University, Northridge. He was born in Los Angeles and lives in Manhattan with his wife, Amy, and his son, Asher.